Reviews of
Where the Heart Is: A Celebration of Home
Edited by Julienne Bennet and Mimi Luebbermann

"Truly a celebration of Spirit's sheltering arms, this sensitive collection of thoughtful writings on the experience of home makes us feel at peace in the midst of change, fragmentation, and tumult. What comes across is the all-pervasive presence of the divine wherever we call home, whether it's a cozy farm in Vermont, grandmother's elm tree, a drifting houseboat, or something intangible that is simply an inward recognition of our own true essence. The editors urge us to think of home as a symbol for nurturing, comforting, and creating beauty, and to commit our lives to sheltering and caring for one another."

— *Science of Mind*

"I have never been so moved and inspired to honor and develop my sense of home — an ideal housewarming gift! The book was a welcome understanding and helpful friend when I needed one, and I recommend it to anyone who has a home — or wants to create one."

— Mary Buckley, *New Dimensions*

"The writings, while each unique, all seem to share a common thread which unites spirit and homelife, a sense that through the creation of "home" our lives are richer, fuller, more alive with meaning. This is a beautiful little book — a perfect gift . . . full of thoughtful writings that are just the right length for momentary pondering."

— *Isabella*

"This book is a delight. Some of the experiences are touching and others are harrowing. But the positive aspects of making 'home' a real part of their lives is what remains. And that is something just about anyone can relate to."

— *Small Press: The Magazine of Independent Publishing*

"This thoughtful book is a meditation on the subject of home from a surprising array of voices."

— *Anderson's Bookshops Newsletter*

"If you feel married to your house — happily or unhappily — *Where the Heart Is: A Celebration of Home* will feel as though it's written just for you."

— *San Jose Mercury News*

"That which makes us feel at home varies with person and circumstance, and becomes clear in this collection of over 100 short anecdotes on the meaning and experience of home . . . A lovely book; a nice housewarming gift."

— *The Phoenix*

"The home is an integral part of our social fabric, and this book celebrates its many meanings."

— *New Age Retailer*

"A thought-provoking, intimate reflection on the many meanings of home."

— *UMBA* newsletter

WHERE

the HEART

IS

A CELEBRATION OF *Home*

WHERE THE HEART IS

A CELEBRATION OF Home

EDITED BY Julienne Bennett and Mimi Luebbermann

ILLUSTRATIONS BY Marlene McLoughlin

PREFACE BY Kent Nerburn
INTRODUCTION BY Mollie Katzen
AFTERWORD BY John Welwood

Wildcat Canyon Press Berkeley, California   New World Library Novato, California

© 1995 Julienne Bennett and Mimi Luebbermann

Co-published by:
Editorial Office
Wildcat Canyon Press
2716 Ninth Street
Berkeley, CA 94710

Distribution Office
New World Library
14 Pamaron Way
Novato, CA 94949

First printing January 1995

Library of Congress Cataloging-in-Publication Data

Where the heart is: a celebration of home/edited by
Julienne Bennett and Mimi Luebbermann.
p.   cm.
Includes index
ISBN 1-885171-00-5: $11.95
1. Home — Psychological aspects.   2. Personal space.
I. Bennett, Julienne, 1954–   II. Luebbermann, Mimi.
HO518.W38   1995
304.2'3 — dc20   94-33971
CIP

Distributed to the trade by Publishers Group West
10 9 8 7 6 5 4 3 2

This book is dedicated to
all those who make their own homes
sanctuaries of peace and safety,
who work to make their communities
better places to live,
and who help to conserve and protect this planet
for all the creatures who call it home.

And, if wishes were houses, may everyone on this earth have
a decent, clean, safe place to live.

A heartfelt thanks to:

Marc Allen
Molly Bennett
Roy Carlisle
Rabbi Steven A. Chester
Judith Fein
Gloria Frym
Susan Gluck
Peter Graves
Nancy Higham and her second grade class at the Higham Family
School
Leslie Henriques
Madelyn Hodges and her one room school, Union Elementary
Barbara Marx Hubbard
Kirk Johnson
Margie McAneny
Dayna Macy
Joel Mackey
Meridith Moraine
Melissa Mytinger
Ellen Peskin
Lory Poulson
Deborah Whitney Prince
Janet Roseman
Eve Rothenberg
Diane Simoneau and her second grade class at the Sierra School
Sharon Smith
Holly Taines
Jim Terr
Tamara Traeder
J. J. Wilson

And a very special thanks to Susan Johnson

TABLE OF CONTENTS

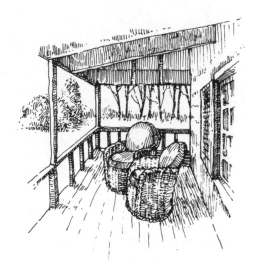

Preface

There is, perhaps, no simpler yet more profound human experience than the experience of home. It is something that is unique to each of us, yet common to us all. And though we all know it in our hearts, it is hard to describe, impossible to define. Like the experience of love or God, it is a shaft of light that enters our lives, and we do it more honor by celebrating its presence than by trying to contain it in words.

Yet words are the brush with which most of us paint when we are trying to share our feelings with others. And it is through words that this book tries to paint us a picture of home, as lived, loved, longed for, and lost, by people of all backgrounds and walks of life. It is a daunting and noble undertaking.

When I was asked to write an introductory piece to this book, I cast about for a way into the subject. I considered framing it in some broad philosophical position, or trying to offer up some deep analysis. But both approaches seemed wrong. Something about home is more full of poetry than philosophy, more filled with love than analysis. I found myself putting aside thought after thought and returning in my heart to those places that rested in my memory, where I had known peace and love and to which I had returned in times of stress and turmoil in my life. And I realized that the place where I had to begin wasn't itself a place at all. It was an old cap that I had carried everywhere with me in my middle teens.

The cap was nothing special. It was one of those old motor pool fatigue caps—olive green and made of soft canvas so that a GI could stuff it into his pocket when he crawled under a tank or a truck.

I would take the cap with me as I wandered among the groves of oak and maple and pine that speckled the landscape near where I lived. After I had walked awhile, I would situate myself under a congenial tree, lay back, and pull the brim of that cap down over my eyes. In my mind's eye I imagined myself as I would be seen by a passerby—laconic, casual, slouched, a devil-may-care James Dean of a youth with all the strength and loose-limbed freedom of a GI on holiday.

But from within, I would stare at the brim of that cap and say to myself, "With this cap, I can live anywhere. When I pull it down over my eyes, I am enclosed in my own little world. What goes on outside does not affect me. I am at home."

It was an ostrich's conceit, to be sure, and one born in no small measure from the delusion that from the outside I presented the rawboned appearance of invulnerability and unassailable strength. But no matter, it worked. Whenever I sat down to rest, on a city park bench or in a field in the country, I would pull that cap down over my eyes, and I was at home.

That cap contained a lesson, though I didn't know it at the time. While I was telling myself that the cap set me free and allowed me to make a home wherever I found myself, in truth I was discovering that to me, home, no matter how temporary, is ever and always a place. It is a part of the landscape where the world seems familiar and there is a sense of rest and peace, and this place is ours to make and remake in every moment, at every stage, throughout our life.

This belief has never left me. It guided me in my younger days when I lived in the back of a van and struggled with the questions of where I was going, both literally and figuratively, with my life.

It guided me as I lived in houses in run-down city neighborhoods, in cabins deep in the Oregon woods, in cold-water garret rooms in small German towns, on Italian mountainsides, and in all manner of other places that I have had occasion to call home in the course of my life.

And it guides me as I meet those on other paths in life, in mansions, in trailers, in hobo jungles, in sprawling ramblers on curving streets.

It makes me see and value home as a place that is shaped into a moment of meaning, and to respect it not for its quality, but for the love with which it is invested and the peace that it provides.

I remember a man who lived in a cardboard box in my neighborhood when I went to graduate school. He had a sleeping bag, a lantern, several books of deranged dogma, and a boy scout pack filled with various items that he considered the necessities of life. He was quite happy, and more than once invited me into his home to share a cup of tea or to listen to some unintelligible rant on the origins of the cosmos or the shape of the coming millennium. It was cramped in his box and it was strange, but it was his home and I felt welcomed and at peace.

Conversely, I have gone into nursing homes where the halls are clean and the walls are white, where all needs are met and no privation exists, and felt a sense of screaming outrage at the homelessness of those whose lives are carried on within them.

By all appearances, their world is no worse and in many ways is much better than my mad friend's cardboard box. Their sheets are fresh; their beds are warm; someone waits upon their every need. But the space they are given has no sense of spiritual boundary, no subtle but actual frame that they can invest with love.

And that, to me, is the issue: home, in its most elementary terms, is a place you can invest with love. It can be a mansion, a heating grate, a cardboard box, or the bill of a GI cap. It need not have shutters or a garden or a swinging white gate. It only needs to have love, and it only needs to provide peace.

I know this is a simple claim. There are those who would say that the child living under a hail of bombs or in a parched land of pestilence and fear can know no peace, and thus can know no home. And there are those of more elevated vision who say that by our very nature we are destined to be homeless, that we carry within us dim presentiments of eternity and can never know a home until we have returned to the state of timeless unity from which we have come.

I would not argue with either of these views. In some way, both are right. But we human beings are resilient creatures, and, at heart, common kin to the birds in the sky and the beasts on the earth. It is in our nature to find a small corner of the earth to mark and claim and invest with the order and familiarity that makes it in some small measure a home.

It may not be the home of our dreams; it may not even be a home that we can claim for more than a moment. But it is a home, nonetheless. And even the mystics among us must turn once or twice, sweep the stones from the earth, and give a minor sense of order to the ground where they choose to lie. And in so doing, they are consecrating, however minimally, the plot of earth where they choose to lay their heads.

Perhaps that is the word that I am seeking. Consecration. To make sacred. Home is the place we make sacred, in memory, in dream, in adjusting the rocks beneath us so that we may sleep a night in comfort. It is not a great, symphonic consecration, calling down the Godhead to participate in our lives. It is a simple consecration of thanks, that we may order and under-stand and rest.

As you read the passages in this book, look to the ways that others have consecrated the spaces in their lives. Look for those whose experience of home need be no more than the feel or texture of an old bowl, the caressing touch of gentle memories. Look for those who have tied their sense of home to a special place: a single house, a piece of land. Imagine those for whom the struggle to make home is a daily task, and pay heed to the searchings of those who see home as a place they have lost or a place they have not yet found.

And look closely to yourself. See what you consecrate. See how you have hallowed the spaces that have been called home in your life. Look not just to the buildings or the plots of land, but to the creak of a certain door, the warmth of a special bed, the corner of a room where the sunlight cascades across a patch of wooden floor. These are the common places that make up our experience of home.

This book is a celebration of these common places. It is a reminder to each of us that the simplest moments and the least expected places can be invested with a special grace, and that it is up to each of us to find these moments and these places, to make them, to acknowledge them, and to honor them.

May the words of this book help you discover those places of love in your life. May they remind you that home—the home you have, the home you only remember, the home that may exist only in your dreams—is not a place you find, but a place you make. It is the place where the ordinary brushes against the sacred, and it is yours to shape, from the commonest of clay, if only you invest your touch with love.

Kent Nerburn holds a Ph.D. in religion and art and is an internationally recognized sculptor with works in such settings as the Peace Museum in Hiroshima, Japan. He has worked among the Ojibwe Indians in Northern Minnesota collecting oral histories and is the author of *Letters to My Son*, *Neither Wolf nor Dog* and numerous other works on Native American culture. He lives with his wife and family in Bemidji, Minnesota.

INTRODUCTION

As I sat down to begin this piece about home, I realized that it was right in the middle of the Jewish festival of Sukkot, the Feast of Tabernacles. I find it fascinating that this thanksgiving festival is so joyful even as it commemorates the years of homelessness and desert wandering suffered by the Hebrews on their way out of bondage in ancient Egypt. We celebrate the "sukkot," the temporary thatch-roofed huts in which our ancestors lived for only a few nights at a time as they wandered for decades without a home. We are instructed to build little replicas of these huts in our own backyards and to dwell in them for a week, so as not to take our comforts for granted. How is it—why is it—that our festival of thanksgiving is organized around the experience of being homeless? Why is it that this joyous occasion focuses on the experience, the comforts, of sheer survival? I think what this peculiar but inspiring celebration teaches us is that where we ultimately dwell is in our life, and in our love for and nurturing of one another, and that this is indeed something for which to be grateful. Although I never got to meet my great grandparents, I picture them in their old-world village knowing this on a deep level and I experience them teaching me these things even now, unimaginable to them as my modern American life would be.

I love stories of my forebears' lives in the shtetls of eastern Europe, where children were raised by whole villages and people lived broadly interconnected lives. Whenever there was a wedding in one family, everyone in the village would come with food to celebrate. If there was a funeral, everyone would show up—again with food—to collectively offer comfort and to keep anyone from ever mourning alone. "Home" in old cultures was defined as a whole community—a network of relationships.

In some ways, my early childhood in upstate New York in the 1950s shared some of these traits. I knew the names of every resident on our street, and there were always people at home, no matter what time of day. Houses were never locked—not even at night. (In retrospect I think that many people didn't even have keys.) The children were free to roam everywhere, largely unsupervised, although always within shouting distance of some-one's mother. "Home" was the entire neighborhood.

In a pattern typical of that time, my father "worked" and my mother "stayed at home." Even though what she did was referred to as "not work-ing," she worked around the clock; she was a veritable one-woman service industry. She was a homemaker, and what she made was a heart and soul for our home; her job was as simple (and, as I later learned, as complex) as that. She took care of us and made us feel loved. I didn't like all the food she cooked, but I loved the fact that she cooked it with her own hands. I didn't like being sent to bed while it was still light outside during daylight savings time, but I loved the fact that there were always crisp, clean sheets on my bed and that she had painted my bedroom walls bright yellow at my request.

I didn't care that my mom didn't wear high heels and nylons to vacuum the house like Harriet Nelson did on TV, nor that she was as often grumpy as she was smiling. I just basked in feeling cared for when she brought me home early from second grade the day I had a fever, and when she didn't yell at me when I lost a dime on the sidewalk, but just gave me another one.

I decided that I wanted to be like my mom, and to become a provider of comfort and safety—a homemaker—for smaller, dependent creatures. I got very busy making a little cardboard home and cigar box bed for Alice, my one and only doll, and I somehow convinced my two toddler brothers that they were puppies, and made pretend dog food for them and a doghouse out of chairs. Most important of all were my invisible tiny friends who flew from outer space into my backyard. I made homes for them by poking holes into the shabby rock foundation of our house and sticking leaves and grass into the holes, and I went outside to feed them every day, even when it rained. I worried about them all the time. I loved the fact that they needed me and that I could provide homes for them.

I wanted to give something back to my mother to reciprocate her nurturing and caretaking in some effective way. When I was seven, I learned how to assemble the Tinkertoy-like innards of our glass percolator and how to measure the coffee with the little spoon, fill the pot up to the line with water, set the timer, and turn the heat down to just the right simmer. Thereafter on most mornings, I got up early and had a freshly brewed pot of coffee ready and waiting for my parents when they came downstairs. I felt proud and important: I was contributing to making a home for my parents, just as they made a home for me and my brothers.

Why do I remember these details so vividly thirty-five plus years later? Why are these the stories that spring to mind when I sit down to write an introduction to an anthology about the concept of home? My mother gave me an example of reaching out and bringing comfort, the essence of home, to others. It is not a coincidence that I grew up to be a cookbook writer and cooking teacher, as well as a writer and painter. To me, these endeavors are all about nurturing, providing, creating beauty, sharing ideas. In the present-day world of mobility, fragmentation, and alienation, where old-world village life as well as the neighborhood communities of just a decade or two ago are becoming distant memories, these concepts are more precious and urgent. We feel most at home in our memories of connection to others, and we yearn to bring back a certain simplicity of basic belonging and acceptance, as well as an appreciation for life itself, taught to us so poignantly by the festival of Sukkot.

The moving testimonials presented in this thoughtfully assembled volume reflect the many new ways in which we are defining and experiencing our relationships to our houses and neighborhoods. They also explore the spiritual links among us, and between all of us and the earth, the home we all ultimately share. Challenging and difficult as these considerations may be, they are also an exciting affirmation of all that is positive about our inter-dependency and cooperative instincts as human beings. As traditional nurturing roles shift, we can all have the opportunity to be homemakers, in the most profound sense, for one another. I hope the thoughts expressed in these pages will open many eyes and minds, inspiring us to commit our lives to sheltering and caring for one another, whether in large or small ways.

Mollie Katzen, a writer and painter, is the author of a series of best-selling cookbooks, including *Moosewood Cookbook*, *The Enchanted Broccoli Forest*, *Still Life With Menu*, and *Pretend Soup*. Her home in northern California, which she shares with her husband, son, and daughter, also contains her painting studio, writing office, and recipe-testing kitchen. She is almost always there.

HOME

AS

PLACE

Be it ever so humble, there is no place like home.

English Proverb, circa 1300's

Home is a Place

"To me home sometimes means fun, and playing, cozy and
loving. Other times screaming and fighting, mad and unhappy.
And always my hamster, Sparky, Sophie, my dog, Mommy,
Daddy, Gabe, my brother, and sometimes friends. I always
feel safe at home."

Mollie Wolf, age eight

"When I think of home, I think of my grandparents' house in
Savonlinna, Finland. I live in California, and I really love my
home, but when I think of 'home,' it's Finland: a homemade
swing hanging from a tree, a rock bowl surrounded by red cur-
rant bushes and ferns, islands, five-hundred-year-old castles."

Kai Groves, age eleven

"I think maybe my true home is my room. I can go in there
and shut the door if my sister is annoying me or if I'm just plain
annoyed. In my room I turn on my radio and plop down with a
book. I forget about the chaos outside my door until someone
comes knocking on that door asking to borrow this or that or
telling me to clean up my junk in the living room."

Molly Bennett, age sixteen

"Home to me is not just a roof over my head, but a dream. If I lost my home it would be like losing all my thoughts, dreams, and memories. I love everything about it, from the north of the house to the south of the house. From the east of the house to the west of the house. If a fire burned down my house, the tears would roll down my face like the water down dirty windows."

Allison Slater, age nine

"At home I can take off those tight and restricting school clothes and walk around in an old T-shirt with stains in the armpits and my ten-year-old jeans with holes in the knees. Home is a place to be myself."

Emily Bennett, age fourteen

"Home is a place where I can sleep in my bed. When I come home my dog Coffee jumps on me. My brother Peter has pillow fights with me."

Andrew Koretz, age eight

3

Georgia

 The origin of my home feeling travels back across the Mississippi to a hot smell. Not the odor of one thing or another, but the particular smell of heat itself. A sticky, invisible, ineluctable thing that whispered and raged that we were alive—humans, dogs, cats, mules, and goats; kudzu weed that threatened to bury the asphalt; profusions of willows, pines, ants, hornets, chiggers, and flies; not to mention the perspiring cars, wood, brick, and glass; organic and inorganic; even what was dead, man-made, and inanimate. As a conduit and tocsin, heat carried that mystic message through Little Five Points and Buckhead and Buttermilk Bottom and me.

Everything was brimming, not only with the redolent smells of itself but with this additional heat thing. And not only the creatures and things we could see, but the air itself was so thick with aliveness that it was hard to sleep, hard to breathe. It wet the sheets, and at night all species collapsed on beds, floors, lawns, and yards, pretending they were doing something other than sweating. Fans only stirred it around like a fork in a pan of hot grease, and air-conditioning was rare. Everything was sweating out of its existence in the heat, as if that were its meaning, sweating

Before the advent of automobiles, it was common for travelers to slice a small sliver from the lintel of their front door and carry it with them on their journey. This act ensured that they would return safely and their house would still be standing when they came home.

away some of its aliveness, and part of the smell was the work of resistance, straight through summer into late fall.

Through the thick vaporous Georgia nights of my youth, I lay in bed, inhaling the fresh hot smell of the bottom sheet like a biscuit, listening to the radio which sounded hot with its dirty midnight lyrics, rolling my tongue around my lips, using the saliva to cool myself off. I rested my hands on the flat surface of my belly where sweat beads festooned my navel. I listened to the moths fry themselves on the porch light over the stoop, heard the sizzling buzz of night beyond the walls and windows, burrowed into my cocoon of heat. Alive, alive.

Happy is the house
that shelters a friend.
Ralph Waldo Emerson

Summer Brenner has been "at home" in cities, deserts, and jungles, on mountains, and at the sea. Currently, she makes her home in northern California. She has two children and is the author of five books of poems and stories, including *The Soft Room, Dancer and the Dance* and *One Minute Movies*.

Home for a Moment

 Leaning back on the heels of my hands, I can hear the horses banging out of their shoots, a Willie Nelson song, and an announcer yelling half in English, half in Shoshone over the tinny P.A. system at the rodeo grounds. I am sitting opposite the door to our nylon tent. It is facing east, planted next to a grove of trees like the rest of the tepees and tents around us. The sun overhead makes the shade under the cottonwood tree feel good. In a few weeks, the old men will fix up the Sundance lodge and the dancers will help the sun rise and set.

As I look west toward the mountains, suddenly, immediately, they seem very big, like I could just take two steps and be right there next to them. They are deep dark green, alive from the melted spring snow. I can see Bear's Ears Peak way back behind all the other peaks, and though it is the middle of summer, there snow is still caught on her ears. The sky along the mountains is big and deep blue, and the clouds resting in the blue are puffy lazy-day clouds with shadows on their bellies. The smell of greasy fry bread, tender new prairie sage, and sweet horse sweat is around me. I am home, for this moment, I am completely back home.

Teri Greeves is a Kiowa Indian who grew up on the Shoshone and Arapahoe Reservation in Wyoming. Around 1680, the Kiowa migrated from this mountainous area to Oklahoma, their present home. She says she will always carry the inherited mountain landscape in her heart.

A Place with Seasons

 I come from a place with seasons—seasons that announce themselves with the certainty of an Arctic cold front. A place where winter is long and rain-sodden, where spring comes on a warm wind rich with the smell of growing things, where the heat of summer turns the hillsides golden brown. Fall arrives with a sudden chill, with fog rolling in over the coastal mountains. In the woods, leaves turn yellow and red, then fall to the ground where they'll make a mulch for spring.

My new home is southern California. We have seasons here too—it's just that they are topsy-turvy, seasons no northern émigré would recognize. The Kumeyaay Indians of the San Diego region had their own way of marking the seasons' passage. Using pictographs or stone markers, they could predict the movements of the sun. On Viejas Mountain, for example, there was a T-shaped arrangement of stones that pointed to a nearby peak to the southeast. On the winter solstice, the sun would rise directly behind that peak. Each year, the Kumeyaay trekked to the top of the mountain to observe the solstice dawn, celebrating the sun's arrival with dance and song. At this time of year, they would say, "The sun is in its home."

Similar markers were located throughout southern California and Baja. It's said that by accurately predicting the solstice, the

Home is the place you can go when you're whipped.
Muhammad Ali

Kumeyaay reassured themselves that the days would not continue to grow shorter until all was dark, but that the sun would return and life would renew itself. Perhaps they were also telling themselves that time passes, that life is nothing but impermanence and change.

Lacking these rituals, it's easy for a southern Californian to ignore the passage of seasons and of time. This is the land of eternal summer, where no one ever grows old.

And still, the years go by. My twenties escaped me like wisps of smoke. Just graduated from college, life seemed to stretch ahead of me like an unchartable highway, one that would go on forever. Somewhere late in that decade I slowly realized that I was, as David Quammen puts it, "spending real currency, hard and finite…the currency of time, energy, stamina." Each year rolled around with few landmarks along the way, the calendar telling me one thing, my body another. The holidays arrived, inevitably too soon. Just as I was getting used to the old year, it was time to usher in a new one. Here I am, in my thirties, wondering where the time has gone.

Would it have been different if I had lived farther north, where I could keep time by the regular process of the seasons? I'm not sure. I do know that very little contemplation has gone on in the

The ancient Romans associated the left side with evil. Anyone entering their house with the left foot brought in evil. A slave, or "footman," was stationed at the door to assure that everyone entered with their right foot first.

past ten years—very little fall composting, if you will. And little spring renewal, either. I've spent the last decade in that eternal stasis of summer.

Now, I want to feel the turn of the seasons in my bones. I want to see my breath at noon, feel the chill of the north wind, and listen to the silence of the dead of the year. I want to watch the migrating birds, and long to follow them south, yet know that I am in my place and that there is no eternal summer for me. The sun is in its home, and so am I. Like the year that is shutting down, my time will come, but not this year or, I hope, the next one or the one after that. I'll go on to see another spring, another rebirth, another summer filled with long hot days, and another fall like this one. But for now, it's time to dig down deep, to burrow under the covers on cold mornings, to compost the chaff of this year's harvest and make a mulch for the coming year. Out of the death of fall and the silence of winter springs new life, new hope.

Lawrence Hogue recently left southern California to enroll in the M.F.A. writing program at the University of Montana and now lives in Missoula. Strangely, he says, he finds himself homesick for California.

The advantage of a hotel is that it's a refuge from home life.
George Bernard Shaw

In My Heart and on the Map

I have lived for the last ten years in Chicago, but my home will always be Mount Vernon, Iowa, a small college town of three thousand in the eastern part of the state just twenty miles north of Iowa City. Although I stay in my parents' house, it's the town that is my home. This is confirmed when I run into people back home who all seem to ask first, "How long you home for?" and only then, "You staying with your folks?"

After being away for awhile, someone who regards a single house as a home might feel a desire to revisit every room or to rummage through a box in a closet. I go to the local clothing store and buy a pair of socks.

Mark Suchomel lives in Chicago in a house that used to be a corner store that served the neighborhood. It is made of bricks and is boxlike, and he has lived there for more than ten years.

It comes to me every day of my life that a home spirit is being awakened amongst us, that as a nation we are beginning to realize how important it is to have homes of our own, homes that we like, that we have been instrumental in building, that we will want to have belong to our children.

Gustav Stickley

My Spot

Bugsy the cat is stretched out full-length, belly up, in the parallelogram of Sausalito sunlight on the carpet. Squint-eyed cat smile.

In one of my clearest memories of early childhood—long before I knew the word "parallelogram"—I sprawl on the carpet in the dining room of our little house in Minneapolis, mid-morning winter sun streaming through the window. I love the sunbeam. I bask in it, swirl the thousands of sparkling specks of dust with fingers, arms, and breath. I have the Sunday funnies spread out in the bright parallelogram on the floor. I lie on the paper and drink in the vivid primary colors of the comics. To this day, my Sunday-paper ritual requires that I wait until the sun comes through the window so that I can spread out the funnies in that bright parallelogram.

This is what home has always felt like, wherever it has been. My bright spot. Easy, comfortable, entertaining, secure. My refuge, my retreat. My territory in the sun.

Me and Bugsy the cat.

Ah! There is nothing like staying at home for real comfort.
Jane Austen,
Emma

Mark Siegel is a writer, sculptor, and creature maker. He published a short story for children called "The Biggest Show on Mars." He lives in Sausalito, California.

Coming Back

It was early spring in Cloud County, Kansas. My friend Ann and I, on our way across the country, had stopped in the town of Clyde to visit her old Uncle Earl. From the house in town where we stayed, we drove with Earl out to the farm that had been his home for most of his life. There we explored the abandoned farmhouse, and I climbed part way up the frame of the windmill to look out across the new wheat flowing in the fields, a tide of short, bright-green blades whipped into ripples and torrents by the wind.

Back in town, we ate in the cafes and stood on the corners talking to neighbors, and in the midst of this homely activity I was surprised to find the experience of my own Midwestern past arising in me. At moments I was caught in wondering sadness, then lifted by a joy that had nothing to do with the circumstances, or held in a listening that sharpened my senses almost to the point of pain. I had not anticipated this awakening, for my native Ohio is situated in a kind of Midwest very different from this prairie state of Kansas. But the people of Clyde were known to me; the land, the smells, the thousand details of ordinary life were familiar. For the first time in twenty years I felt drawn to the region of my growing up.

Comfort to me is a room that works for you and your guests. It's deep upholstered furniture. It's also knowing that if someone pulls up a chair for a talk, the whole room doesn't fall apart. I'm tired of contrived decorating.

Billy Baldwin,
from *Home: A Short*
History of An Idea

And so I began to understand that the land of my childhood lived in me as vividly as the urban California place and customs in which I now exist. The great flat midland that had cradled my becoming, that was my first home, rang me like a bell, awakening me.

Sandy Boucher lives with her partner in a yellow house on a street between two freeways in Oakland, California. She is the author of *Turning the Wheel: American Women Creating the New Buddhism* and is currently working on her fifth book, which explores mid-life issues for women.

An early American tradition that some say dates back to the Druids is to hang a young sapling tree at the highest point in a newly erected house or barn. It was traditionally done at the end of a house or barn "raising" and was intended to apologize to all the trees that were killed to build the structure and to symbolize new life.

13

The Lake

 My fondest memories of home are based on the only vacations I knew as a young girl—going up to "the lake" in northern Minnesota. We changed lakes and changed resorts over the years, but they all had a comfortable sameness about them that felt like a homecoming. The wooden dock always sagged and always smelled wet and musty. The cottage always had plaid bedspreads and an aluminum coffeepot and a deck of cards hidden in the kitchen drawer. We always made popcorn, went fishing, and did all the things we never had time for at home. It all took hold of me in a way I'm only dimly beginning to realize.

Louise Mengelkoch is a journalist teaching at Bemidji State University in Minnesota. She is the co-editor of *Native American Wisdom,* and has been published in numerous newspapers and magazines, including *The Columbia Journalism Review.*

The strands are all there; to the memory nothing is ever lost.
Eudora Welty

I Always Had to Leave

 I live in a hotel now, but I don't consider that my home. I grew up with foster parents and a foster brother and sister. But that wasn't home to me. I wouldn't stay in one place. I always had to leave. I'd just take off and start walking and I ended up where I ended up, one time in San Diego, one time in Palo Alto.

I always wanted to be outside, so I guess outside feels more like home than inside. When I was living in People's Park I felt that was my home. I lived there for fourteen years. I just recently moved out about five months ago. I had a lot of friends there. I used to hang out with them, drink a lot, party a lot. We were all like brothers and sisters living together, for years.

The hotel room doesn't feel like home. It's inside. It's not in my nature to be inside. The manager said I can't have any of my friends over because most of my friends are alcoholics. They start drinking and get in fights and get in trouble. So I can't have that anymore. Most of the time I'm by myself. I guess if I'm there longer I'll consider it my home.

When it gets cold and rainy, that just happens. It doesn't really bother me. It takes a lot for me to get cold. It has to be real, real cold for me to feel cold.

A home is not a mere transient shelter; its essence lies in its permanence, in its capacity of accretion and solidification, in its quality of representing, in all its details, the personalities of the people who live in it.

H. L. Mencken

Tere Charging Thunder lives in Berkeley, California.

An Icy Arctic Home

 Before all else, home is a specific place on the earth. Home is an environment, a climate, a geography, and a cultural history. When I was a child, I puzzled why the Inuit chose to remain in their icy, Arctic home. Why did they stay in the frigid north where their forefathers had lived, hunted, and died instead of moving to the easier living of the warmer south?

It's no wonder that I didn't understand the unbreakable attachment the Inuit felt for their home, their native place on earth. As Americans, we have been taught that easy mobility is a virtue, that the ties that bind us to place are a constriction, a fettering of our freedom. If it's easy for us to pull up our roots, that may simply mean that our roots are shallow. The Inuit chose to stay in the north because they were rooted in their homeland. It wasn't bondage, it wasn't a sacrifice, it wasn't inconvenient. It was home.

Steven Gorelick was a "Navy brat" whose early childhood was divided among five states and two continents. Today he lives in Berkeley, California, where he runs the North American office of the International Society for Ecology and Culture.

To us, the ashes of our ancestors are sacred, and their resting place is hallowed ground. You wander far from the graves of your ancestors, and seemingly without regret.

Chief Seattle

The Neighborhood

 I moved around a lot in my life, but when my marriage ended and I was on my own with two small children, it was time to settle in one place. I had to work two jobs most of the time to make ends meet, and the children needed a neighborhood where everyone knew them, including the food market owner and the local cop. So I settled on a corner in the upper west side of Manhattan.

We've moved twice since then, but only a few doors one way or the other, always keeping the same neighborhood. I know almost every face on the street, and I know all the dogs. I know when the cute young woman on the block is dating, because a cute young guy walks her dog in the morning. I ask the World War II vet (whose dog finally died of old age a few years ago) how his foot is feeling. I give the ladies who sell used clothes on the weekend some of my recycled clothes for them to hang on the school fence, and a year later I recognize the coat or blouse that someone else is wearing.

Some people think of New York as an enormous, unfriendly city, but to me it's a neighborhood town. It's my home.

Barbara Sher is the author of *Wishcraft* and *I Could Do Anything If I Only Knew What It Was*. She is an internationally known writer, teacher, and lecturer. She says she loves her apartment, her building, her neighborhood, and all her friends and neighbors in New York.

Let the street be as wide as the height of the houses.
Leonardo Da Vinci

Buyers are Liars

There is a saying in real estate that buyers are liars. New clients tell us what they are looking for in a house, and inevitably, when they buy something, it is not what they described. Yet most buyers say the same thing: "We knew the minute we walked into this house that this was the one. This was where we were supposed to live."

Buying a house is one of the biggest decisions that most of us will make, and there is a lot more involved than just the business transaction. Houses aren't just concrete and steel and wood and plaster and paint. They have their own spirit.

Houses are alive, and I believe that they have memories of the nails that were driven, all of the people who have walked over the threshold, all of the storms they have weathered, all of the love and laughter of the people who have lived in the house. That's why a person can walk into a house and feel an immediate attraction. It's like meeting an old friend again, or the sense of chemistry you feel with a new love.

I think it's not just the people finding a new house, but it's also the house finding new people. Someone may walk into a house with an emotional wound or a deficiency of some kind, and the house seems to communicate to that person that it holds something healing, something fulfilling for them.

The fellow that owns his own home is always just coming out of a hardware store.

Frank McKinney Hubbard

It works the opposite way too. Sometimes clients describe in great detail what they want in a house and I'll find three houses that are a perfect fit. When I show them each house, frequently they'll walk in and say, "I don't know why it's wrong, it's just wrong, we just don't like it." I think the personality of the house and the personality of the buyer clash.

It's not just you, and it's not just the house. When a house is on the market, it doesn't matter how weird it is, in what stage of disrepair it might be, or how bizarre the floor plan is. A buyer always comes who loves that house. Always.

For some new owners, a house holds out a certain promise. Home represents to them what they want to become. Frequently clients say, "We could convert the basement, we could have a studio here, we could rent out the cottage, we could have a gourmet kitchen, we could have a nursery for our baby." They mean: *We could live that life, and we could become that kind of people.* Sometimes their dreams don't come true, and they simply live in the space without changing it. But often people actually do live out their dreams, and it's a beautiful sight to see.

Holly L. Rose has worked as a realtor in Berkeley, California, for five years helping her clients successfully buy and sell their homes. In her previous life, she was a scientist.

*And of all man's felicities
The very subtlest one, say I,
Is when for the first time he sees
His hearthfire smoke against the sky.*
Christopher Morley

The Best Home I've Ever Had

 I hired a coyote (a guide who takes illegals across
the Mexican border) to take me into America in
December 1989. We ran all night, running and run-
ning to find a safe place to cross the line. Finally, about six in the
morning, we crossed over. We had a ride waiting to take us to San
Diego, and along the way we had to wait to cross an immigration
checkpoint. One of the coyotes passed us in another car and drove
through the checkpoint. We waited for word from him at a phone
booth some distance away. When the immigration officials stopped
checking cars—I don't know why, maybe for a coffee break—he
called us on the phone and we zoomed over the line.

I met one of my uncles in Los Angeles and he drove me to the
mountains not far from Stockton. He dropped me off in a trailer
high in the mountains and left me there. When I went inside,
I found that there was almost no food, and the trailer was very
cold. My uncle didn't come back for fifteen days.

I was used to warm temperatures in Mexico, and I had only
brought two shirts, two pairs of pants, two pairs of socks, and two
changes of underwear. The heater was broken and there was only
a small sleeping bag, not enough to keep me warm at night. But I
had learned survival training with the Mexican army, so I made

traps and captured several rabbits and some quail, and I rationed the food that I had.

The first week in the trailer, I wanted to go home. The second week, I began to think that I had to prove myself. What would my friends say if I came home without staying and making a lot of money? The day before Christmas, my uncle came back. He took me to Stockton to meet all my relatives living in America whom I had never met before. They looked at me and said I looked very thin, and I laughed.

My uncle got me a job as a farm worker in the Central Valley. My employer spoke to me in Spanish, and after a year I realized that I wasn't learning English. I was determined to speak the language, for I thought that if I could speak the language I could get a better job. I began to try to speak some English, trying to read the newspapers and pronounce the words I read. After three years in the mountains, I quit my job and moved into town. I got an American girlfriend, and she helped me learn English. I worked in the surrounding fields as a day laborer.

These years were very hard, and I often thought of giving up and going back to Mexico. But I didn't, and eventually I moved to another area where I heard that the living was more peaceful and work more permanent.

Now I work as a gardener and handyman. I make ten dollars an

You walk on carrying on your shoulders a glass door to some house that's not been found. There's no handle. You can't insure it. Can't put it down.

W. S. Merwin

21

hour. Some days, I make $30 and some days I make $60. I like this work better than working in the fields. I came to America to get rich, but I know now that I will never get rich. Still, I speak, read, and write English, and although I work very hard I have a very good life. I have a Mexican girlfriend, and I help her with her son. I have many friends here, from all kinds of lifestyles and many different nationalities. In America, there is some discrimination, and sometimes people call me a dirty Mexican illegal, but it's not like Mexico. Here, people who are rich still talk to me as a friend, and it doesn't matter how much money they have. Perhaps someday I will go back to Mexico, maybe when I retire, but I like it here in America, I think this is the best home I've ever had.

Anonymous

*Away from the world
and its toils
and its cares,
I've a snug little
kingdom up four
pair of stairs.*
William Thackeray

Home Is Where the Stove Is

I used to laugh at my Italian relatives who always wanted to sit in the kitchen. They even built houses without dining rooms. Big kitchens were all they wanted. They lived their whole lives in those kitchens, around the stove, eating, talking, playing cards, reading newspapers, drinking coffee. When they weren't around the stove, they were in church, in God's home, but that's another story.

Home is where the stove is. When I think of all the places I've lived, I think of what I cooked in the kitchen: cheese tarts in Cambridge, beet soup in Berkeley, and shrimp curry in Singapore. Home is where I sauté the garlic and chop the onions, where the frying pan makes music.

An old Russian proverb says, "The oven is the mother." Food, warmth, acceptance, I can find it all at the stove. Who needs any-thing else?

Jo Ann Passariello Deck keeps a holy card of St. Anthony in her desk drawer. She always laughs out loud when she finds "Pasta e Fagioli," standard Friday night fare in her childhood home, on the menus of San Francisco's finest res-taurants.

My kitchen is a mystical place. It is a place where the sounds and the odors carry meaning that transfers from the past and bridges into the future.
Pearl Bailey

City Home

Someone I never met built the tall Victorian house where I live now; dozens more people I will never know have occupied it. Scrubbing and sweeping, I cleaned woodwork and floors, hauling away filth. I laid new rugs over fir floors hidden from sunlight for a generation and peeled away wallpaper older than my mother. When I open my trunks of leather and wool clothing in an upstairs bedroom, the scent of campfires circles against the ceiling. My rifle and beaded bags hang on the walls beside photographs of people I have loved.

At night, I wander this house touching woodwork to find my way. Sometimes I seem to hear whispers from the tenants who boarded in these rooms. My pupils widen to catch the glow of street lamps; George and I used to walk in moonlight around the ground-hugging house we built. My blood and sweat dried in those beams, in the floorboards. Calluses told me where each 2 x 4 stood inside the walls, how each window fit its frame. I chose the colors and painted the walls; I moved each piece of furniture a dozen times and set every book on each shelf. More of George remains in my soul than in the hillside cemetery. In the same way, I was in that house no less than it was in me.

*...we shape
our dwellings,
and afterwards
our dwellings
shape us.*
Sir Winston Churchill

24

Now, hidden in darkness, I feel my way along the passages of a house built about the time my father was born. My fingertips suck its secrets in; my sighs perfume the ceilings with sage smoke. A lamp in my study casts shadows on a kestrel's wing and a Lakota beaded bag in the shape of a turtle. Sometimes I see the glimmer of the computer screen reflected in the empty eye sockets of an owl skull.

Spinning the journal of my life up and down these stairs and corridors, I am making this house mine, for now. My words blend with its ancient creaks and sighs.

Linda Hasselstrom is a writer and rancher. Her books include *Windbreak: A Woman Rancher on the Northern Plains, Land Circle, Going Over East, Dakota Bones, Roadkill, Caught by the Wind*, and the forthcoming *A Roadside History of South Dakota.*

Nobody shoulders a rifle in defense of a boarding house.
Bret Harte

I Still Call It Home

My homeplace is Sibley, Iowa. My parents were born in the county, died and were buried there, along with two young children. The ashes of a son who died years after they did were scattered on their graves. Many generations of my ancestors are buried there, immigrants from Germany, Canada, and Ireland. When I return to Iowa, their spirits accompany me as I walk the streets of my youth.

The park is virtually unchanged since my childhood. I'm certain that the green wooden benches under the trapezes are the same ones I stood on to reach the bars and rings. Back then, after hours of swinging, my arms ached and my hands were sore with open blisters, but it was hard to quit when having fun.

If I was lucky enough to have a nickel in my pocket, I crossed the street to spend it at the Park Grocery. On entering, a bell tinkling over the door would bring Mary Breckle from the back room, wiping her hands on her apron and wearing the scent of Fels Naptha soap on her wrists. Or her husband, Rudy, might step from behind the curtain that separated the store from their parlor. A radio played back there—music, Fibber McGee and Molly, Jack Benny, a soap opera—and enticing cooking odors often wafted out to the store. Today the store is run by another

*"Where is Kansas?"
asked the man,
with surprise.
"I don't know,"
replied Dorothy
sorrowfully,
"but it is my home,
and I'm sure it's
somewhere."*

L. Frank Baum,
The Wizard of Oz

generation of Breckles who expanded the old cottage, keeping the heart and soul of the one-room store started over fifty years ago.

The county courthouse, built in 1902, is on the National Register of Historic Buildings. On the lawn is a granite monument engraved with the names of the local men who served in World War I. As a child, I often stopped there to read my father's name.

The school I attended was destroyed by fire many years ago. Two of the houses in which I lived remain unchanged; the other two have undergone renovation and are recognizable to me only because of their location. The last house we occupied stood along the town's only boulevard, a grassy strip where we kids gathered to play, or to eat after raiding a rhubarb patch, an apple tree, a grapevine, or a tomato garden.

Another favorite gathering place for kids was the alleys that bisected every block. While we played there on summer evenings, housewives roamed up and down, admiring gardens and talking with neighbors about canning and children and weather.

The Palace Cafe is located across the street from where it was when my mother worked there as a cook. One night in 1951 she cooked supper for Henry Fonda and the stage cast of *Mister Roberts,* stranded in town during a train breakdown in a snowstorm.

One place that has not changed is the Max Theater. The new

I have three chairs in my house: one for solitude, two for friendship and three for society.
Henry David Thoreau

27

owner has retained the name and its fifties look—the way it was when I ushered there. Peering through the doors, I can almost smell the popcorn and see Mrs. Max behind the ticket booth. On the other side of the curtained inner door, Mr. Max collected tickets and greeted moviegoers.

Along the boulevard there once stood a house that was, when it was built before the turn of the century, one of the grandest in town. During my childhood it was owned by a reclusive spinster, the daughter of the original owner. She kept the dark green window shades drawn at all times, shrouding the house in mystery and stirring children's imaginations. My friends and I called her "the whale lady" because, for some reason, we believed that she kept a whale in her basement. The house is now gone; after it deteriorated beyond repair, it was burned to the ground in a firefighting exercise.

Across the street from where her house stood, is a parking lot that used to be a block-square grassy area that we kids called the Dog Park. I have no idea why. It was not used as a place to walk dogs; people did not walk dogs in small towns in those days; animals roamed free. During World War II a wooden structure was erected there, bearing the names of county men and women serving in the war. I often stopped to gaze proudly at my two oldest brothers' names and to see whose names had a gold star next to them, indicating that they had died in the war.

They've built an addition to the library where I spent many happy hours. There are now meeting rooms and offices in the old section. Gone are the dictionary so heavy it had to rest on a stand, a rack on which newspapers skewered by metal rods hung upside down, and a globe that stood on the floor and seemed as big as the world itself. They've kept Miss Walton's curved desk, and atop a file cabinet are the stereoscope and double-image picture post-cards that once transported me to exotic lands.

Noticeably absent is something that could not be saved and tucked into a corner. The library once held within its walls a distinctive smell: a combination of old books, book-binding paste, newspaper ink, furniture oil, floor wax, and that dry, dusty odor that steam radiators emit. That aromatic charm must have escaped out the windows and doors during renovation; there is no trace of it now. Except in my memory.

Madonna Dries Christensen is a professional writer who has lived away from her childhood home for thirty-five years, but still thinks of it as home. She lives in Sarasota, Florida.

The phrase "getting out of the wrong side of the bed" usually refers to someone having a bad day, or feeling grumpy or crotchety. This harks back to the superstition that, by going to bed on one side at night and getting up out of the other side in the morning, one formed a protective magic circle. Not to do so was bad luck.

Saying Good-Bye

 My family and I vacationed in Gloucester, a little fishing village on the northeast coast of Massachusetts, every summer when I was a boy. The earliest recollection I have of those summers is of saying good-bye. To the town. It may seem peculiar that I think of home as a place I have left so many times in my life, but I miss Gloucester. She is the place I am always trying to go home to.

I remember sitting in the back of my father's '65 Plymouth wagon and saying good-bye as my father drove off, away from the little motel on the beach where we had spent a week. My two older brothers were in the rear seat, my parents were in front. Being the smallest, I was relegated to the rear compartment with the luggage and the beach chairs and the fishing poles. I was five or six years old. The rear window was down. The car was full of sand. Everything around me smelled like the ocean except for the fishing poles: they just smelled like seaweed. I can still hear the seagulls cry, and I can see the waves fade from view as my father drives away. Away from the ocean. Away from Gloucester.

Each year, we went to that little town for one week in early August. We fished. We ate steamed lobster and corn on the cob and raw clams and flounder. Some days we would just lie on the beach and swim in the surf. My brothers and I would build

*Go home
and say prayers.*

Proverb

enormous sand castles on that beach, great giant fortresses connected by moats and roads and bridges made from discarded popsicle sticks. To me, they were real palaces into which the kings and queens of the beach would come as soon as night fell. Other days my mother would take us to the rocks on the opposite side of town, where we would sit for hours just watching the swells crash against the shore. The surf is amazing in Gloucester, so powerful, so inspiring. Watching it, you become part of it. It hypnotizes you like that. Then, as the sun began its descent down onto the horizon, we would go into town. We would walk past the galleries and the jewelry shops and the art stores and the restaurants, down to the docks where the fleet was moored. There we would stop and watch the artists paint the fishing boats and the men who sailed those boats. We'd stand quietly behind them, making sure we didn't disturb their concentration, while they sketched the seabirds that were kind enough to sit and pose atop the lobster pots. We did this year after year. The same silly things. Watching the artists. Watching the waves. Fishing. Eating. Building castles. And swimming. We did them as a family, and we never seemed to get tired of it. In fact, we seemed to need to go to Gloucester more and more with each passing year. It became like a pilgrimage.

I'm thirty-six now, and I go back to Gloucester as often as I can (which isn't nearly as frequently as I would like). It's the same as it was thirty years ago. It doesn't change. For me, at least.

The smell of that buttered toast simply talked to Toad, and with no uncertain voice; talked of warm kitchens, of breakfasts on bright frosty mornings, of cosy parlour firesides on winter evenings, when one's ramble was over and slippered feet were propped on the fender; of the purring of contented cats, and the twitter of sleepy canaries.

Kenneth Grahame, *The Wind in the Willows*

Gloucester has always been able to transcend time like that. I tell myself that someday I will live in Gloucester and make it my home.

Anyway, we drove off that morning. Nobody said a word. I think we all were moved somehow by the town itself, by what it meant, by how it made us feel just being there for one week. I remember crying. I was so sad to be leaving. What a baby I was, my brothers later told me. I simply told them that I would go back. Someday.

Carl Adam Richmond lives in southern New England, where he works as an editorial assistant for Yale University. He is an accomplished poet, the author of several short works of fiction and his autobiography, *Twisted*.

Home is home, be it never so homely.
Proverb

32

Suburban Gardens

 In my childhood, in suburbia, my family owned a single tract of land in the middle of Pennsylvania, bulldozed of all trees and other relics of the past, with a basic brick ranch house set upon it. To my parents, who came from apartments in Harlem where air shafts were the amenities, this was Eden. The garden of Eden. The dream of America. A backyard in the fifties where their kids could run safe in pajamas, catching fireflies in mayonnaise jars with tin foil lids, while they drank iced tea and mint from pitchers on the screened-in patio they built with their own hands. My parents took particular relish in the fact that they grew the wild mint themselves in a useless patch of soil by the back door beside the milkbox. It was behind the garbage cans—a place most people would not think to cultivate. But my parents thought it was the perfect spot for a thorny, gangly mint plant. "They grow like garbage," my father used to laugh, "that's why we planted them here beside the garbage."

Laura Bridenthal doesn't live in suburbia and doesn't have a garden. She lives in a penthouse in San Francisco with a concrete balcony and a view of the ocean.

In violent and chaotic times such as these, our only chance for survival lies in creating our own little islands of sanity and order, in making little havens of our homes.

Sue Kaufman,
Falling Bodies

At Home on the Earth

Housing is a kind of secondary body, a constructed means for being at home on the earth—since evolution has somehow seen fit to make humans, alone among all the animals, unable to nest comfortably in nature. As a child I remember seeing snakes in the grass, fish in the lake, and birds in the trees; then I would turn to our big white house on a hill and wonder, why do we need a house anyway? When I was about five that house burned down entirely. Our dog, a fluffy Spitz who liked to sleep in the pump house underneath the light bulb that kept our water from freezing in the wintertime, somehow managed to push his blanket up against that light bulb late one night, thus starting the fire. So said the firemen.

The dog survived and I was awakened by someone who grabbed my arm and pulled me so hard that I never got on my feet till I was outside; my father had rescued me while my mother crawled under the smoke to get to the telephone. My two sisters had been awakened first when the three small windows on the front door, a few feet from their own closed door, exploded from the heat.

For a while after that our home was a trailer perched on the hillside; I've seen pictures of it but can't recall it. My mother says that I had to be sedated at night for weeks, because tree

The dome of thought,
the palace of the soul.
Lord Byron

branches that scraped on the roof of the trailer would remind me of the fire and I'd wake up screaming. I remember none of this.

My memories of the fire are entirely pleasant: we all went to the neighbors' house in the middle of the night, a truly extraordinary event, and drank hot chocolate and watched a big fire.

A few years later, when we had moved into an exact replica of the house that had burned, my mother caught me setting fire to my bedspread. It scared her so much she didn't spank me; she simply stopped speaking to me for a couple of days. All this I remember vividly.

I remember that the box of matches represented a fascinating question: how much fire did there have to be before it was out of control? What was the most fire I could put out? It was a scientific experiment really, driven by an emotional fixation well beyond my comprehension.

I now have a much better handle on the issue of Promethean control. But fire will probably always be a part of what I look for in a home; I love wood stoves and fireplaces. Something that once made me homeless is now something I prefer to have in my home.

It makes me wonder: can I look around my room and see mementos of other past traumas? Is anyone's home entirely protective, or is a home partially a library of our pains? What makes us feel comfortable may be more complex than we usually

Houses without personality are a series of walled enclosures with furniture standing around in them. Other houses are filled with things of little intrinsic value, even with much that is shabby and yet they have that inviting atmosphere...

Emily Post

35

think. Home is a place to call our own, but the need for it reflects our discomfort at being on the earth in the first place. We try to create a place where we belong, because most of us truly cannot belong, beyond the artifice of a camping trip, in Mother Nature. She seems to have expelled us as a species, at some point, like our own mothers expelled each one of us.

D. Patrick Miller is a native of Charlotte, North Carolina, who bicycled to California in 1976. With the exception of a four-year hiatus in southern California, he has been at home in Berkeley ever since. A senior writer for *Yoga Journal,* Miller is also the author of *A Little Book of Forgiveness.*

The Perch

Everyone has a spot where they feel comfortable and safe. My octogenarian mother called the end of the green velvet Empire couch in the living room her perch. No one else in the family encroached upon it, for it was her sole spot, at the end of two footpaths across the carpet: one from her bedroom to the living room, and the other from the couch to the kitchen and back. Each day she settled at the end of the couch, and it served as her base of operation for twenty years.

As she grew older and walking became more difficult, she spent more time at her perch. Through the three large windows across the room, she could see the front yard and street and the weeping willow tree and the sky. From her perch she watched for the postman, noticed the neighbors, and filled her days with reading and an occasional television program. She loved to have a fire in the grate on cold, cloudy days and shared her perch with the family cat that lay beside her and slept, often in unison with her.

No other place in the house had such profound meaning for her. A lamp on the rosewood table provided light and a wristwatch lay face up to help keep track of time. The perch was constant and she felt safe there.

Tom Adams writes about aging in America. His mother shared the family home with Tom and his son until age 102, when her rich and giving life ended.

Salt purifies, and so it was often used in house blessing ceremonies to cleanse and purify the dwelling. Salt also acts as a preservative, making it a symbol of lasting friendship. As a mark of hospitality, Arabs place salt in front of a stranger to promise their good will.

After Twenty-Five Years, How Do You Say Good-bye?

 It's September and my husband and I have been in our new house for almost three months, a quarter of a year. When we left our old house on Irving Avenue we had been there for a quarter of a *century*, almost exactly twenty-five years, longer than either of us had lived in any other home.

Our first child, Keith, was just sixteen months old when we moved in, a cute little red-haired toddler. He can't remember any other home. Nor can Alexander, who arrived that summer.

Built in 1906, on an elm-lined street one block away from the city's largest lake, the three-story Victorian was our first house and we loved every charming detail. The front hall had dark oak woodwork, a beautiful open stairway, with a carved banister and gracefully turned spindles, and a tall built-in bookcase and mirror. A coat of arms painted in the middle of the mirror had a Latin motto whose meaning we disputed for twenty-five years. My husband always said it meant "Praise the virtue of action." I said it meant "Praise the virtuous deed." We each liked our own translation better, so we never looked it up.

Our favorite part was the wide open porch that ran across the entire front. Our boys grew up, and went off to kindergarten and grade school and high school and college, all from that big front porch. We've said our teary farewells and we've hugged our Welcome Home hugs on that sweet old porch. Two white Adirondack chairs faced the sidewalk, and two giant pots of bright pink geraniums graced the doorway. We'd sit in our chairs and chat with passing neighbors, young and old. The porch was our public living room.

What makes a home? Not the building itself certainly, although every corner of it can grow dear and the light from every window can become a private benediction. A home is the family who lives inside and their life together, the friends who come and go through its doors, the neighbors and the neighborhood that surround it and support it and breathe the very breath of life into it. And yet I'll always think of our house on Irving Avenue as a living, breathing thing, with a pulse and a heartbeat. I'll always think of it as a friend for life.

So, after twenty-five years, how do you say good-bye? On closing day, my husband and my younger son Alexander and I walked through our house, room by room. We said good-bye to each one, starting on the third floor and making our way down to the front door. We laughed and we cried over the little things we remembered happening in each room. At last my husband and I took down the Amish quilt that hung in the living room and folded it

...to leave Coorain was almost beyond my comprehension. Each day I prepared myself for the departure by trying to engrave on my memory images that would not fade—the dogs I loved best, the horse I rode, the household cat, the shapes of trees.

Jill Kerr Conway,
The Road to Coorain

quietly. There was nothing left to do but go. Close the door. Lock the lock.

The dear old place stood empty, clean and ready for its new family, a young couple with a cute little red-haired toddler. It was their first home. I wept for all the memories it held for us. But I loved passing our home on to another family, who would now begin to raise their children, invite their friends in, and store up their own memories in that wonderful old house on Irving Avenue.

Patricia Blakely lives in Minneapolis, Minnesota with her husband in a sunny corner duplex four blocks away from the house they just sold. She looks forward to living in her new home for another quarter of a century.

For the Thief

Thank you for leaving the desk
   and the chair,
the books, snapshots, and piano.
I've heard of moving-van robberies—
coming home from work to the percussion
of empty rooms. Thank you for
leaving the trapped air
that softens the blunt edges of my day.
What's mine—the hum of identity—
still surrounds me,
though the electronics
are gone and the jewelry
that was too precious to wear.
Thank you for not spraying
the walls with Coke or with piss.
Thank you for being a professional,
tidy and quick, entering with a clean
and silent cut, not wasting your time
or mine with vandalism or assault.

When my mother was robbed
the closets and drawers were dumped
on the floor. All that was stolen were
the towels that had hung in her bathroom.
Her neighbors, the police said, had
lost their cookware. Better that our houses
become someone's mall than shooting range.
With my cousins, one took
a knife-blade against the throat.
Another, in Madrid, was dragged three blocks
by her hair. Thank you for knowing
what you were here for, for tending
to your business without rage.

Alison Hawthorne Deming is the director
of the University of Arizona Poetry Center and
the author of *Temporary Homelands* and *Science
and Other Poems*, which was nominated for a
Pulitzer Prize. She really wishes she lived in
a tree house.

When I Was a Little Girl, I Sang

When I was a little girl, I sang. When I was a child, but a child, I sang. I sang songs of this place and my time. I sang about trees, the maples and oaks, covering me, like God, like my father. I sang of the rain, the heavy winds that made Grandmother's elm tree moan. I sang of grey-green light in the grass, a dark sky waiting to drop her waters on my head and in the iris bed and down drainspouts. I sang of porch steps and summer evenings relieved of hot days.

The plane bringing me home lands in fields of corn. It comes from the dry, bristle-brown of the West Coast. The hot green plowed black earth rising up. Hello, green earth, hello. Bring me corn and beefsteak, tomatoes and applesauce and fresh brown cakes. I am home.

My town is crumbling. The paint skins crack, the streets hump and puddle in the rain. The outskirts of town wear new brick houses, a rest home, a few uncertain businesses. The grand homes in the middle of town, the turrets and balconies and sun rooms, those and the town square and the edges of what used to be are where my town is showing her age.

I too am older. I understand parts of you are dying, my town, in the long grasses that cannot conceal foundations that warp and let in vines like the one growing through the bathroom floor and up the rungs of the chair that mother has not moved. The house is crumbling like the town and like parts of me.

Mother says, "You can't get good help anymore. Used to be men came around here looking for jobs. Now they can make more money living off the government. Nobody wants work. This country," mother says, "is in sorry shape."

I think I never saw this town their way. The way of the people I thought belonged. The town cast me out, coughed me up like a foreign particle. That's what I thought. I didn't know that each person's way is alone.

This town that had warm apron laps for my childhood did not have room for me to grow up. I stand before the congregation of those who love Him. Part of the choir that left after graduation, singers looking for new songs. We come back, the men and women who almost grew up here. We circle back to what we loved first. To the unforgotten sustenance, the brick streets, to the town that is slowly shedding its memory.

Marijane Datson is the administrative director for Tale Spinner's Theater, a playwright with the Oral History Playwrights project, a published poet, NEA Award-winning playwright, and a community college writing instructor. She co-founded The Gathering Place, a woman's reading series and book room. She lives in San Francisco, California.

I Remember

I remember,
I remember,
The house where
I was born,
The little window
where the sun
Came peeping in at
morn.

Thomas Hood

Disorder and Clean Dirt

 It's a shame that the popular stereotype for the cleaning lady is still so unflattering. Maybe cleaning ladies should be seen as magical people who have access to areas where the gentry seldom go, under the bed where the dust balls congregate, or behind the kitchen stove where things go to die.

Several years ago I left my profession as a psychotherapist and started a housekeeping business. Since then I have learned more about people than I did in years of clinical training, and in a more compassionate way.

For a house to be a home there must be a certain degree of personal order which may be hard to maintain because of the law of creeping entropy. When this order breaks down, then the house ceases to be a home. Such a house can in fact turn on its owner in ways that are very unpleasant and may result in a terrible loss of self-esteem.

"No I can't invite you in; my house is such a mess!"

"Nothing looks right any more!"

"It's all my fault."

In addition, most neighborhoods have the *clean house* where the clean, happy, well-organized people live, setting standards that ordinary people can never ever achieve. "Oh, if only I could be like Mrs. or Mr. So and So."

When the house is shared, the problems are compounded because each member may see "home" differently. I believe that more quarrels between spouses occur in the kitchen over what "really clean" means than in the bedroom.

As a housekeeper over the years, I have been able to bring a little light into troubled homes and help owners live peacefully with their houses by seeing both points of view. Houses need love and attention just like people do. Consideration and affection can turn a house into a home for life.

One final message. A certain degree of disorder and clean dirt are inevitable and in fact necessary for a house to be really happy. A house that looks lived in is a home.

Patricia Crossman is a licensed psychotherapist, but she calls herself variously a house therapist, a house organizer, or a cleaning lady. She lives in Kensington, California.

In a hole in the ground there lived a hobbit. Not a nasty, dirty, wet hole, filled with the ends of worms and an oozy smell, nor yet a dry, bare, sandy hole with nothing in it to sit down on or to eat: it was a hobbit-hole, and that means comfort.

J.R.R. Tolkien,
The Hobbit

Love at First Sight

 It is raining hard. A small fire thrives in the tiny hearth behind me, and three blossoming plum trees are framed by drafty windows. From time to time I check the ceiling over the old piano, with nine keys still mute from the leak three years ago. It is the third day of rain, and the roof is still holding.

I am a single woman, forty-six, the proud owner in partnership with First Nationwide Mortgage of a small house on a small piece of land worth a huge amount of money. The roof is a time bomb that will cost seventeen thousand dollars to replace when it finally gives way. Last summer's vacation fund paid for one four-day weekend away and four months of exterior painting. Everything I have saved, or been given, or found on the sidewalk has gone into my house, which could be swallowed up in less than a minute by a large earthquake.

Yet the desire to have my own home was so strong, so deep and primitive, that I became irrationally determined to acquire one. I cheerfully ignored concerns like money, time, effort—all blurred by the passion for my own weedy, water-sucking lawn; for my own leaky roof that no one else can ask me to move out from under (except God); for my own prehistoric stove that can be regulated only by opening and closing its door, but which still, miraculously, produces delicate little cakes.

The house has robbed me of time and money I did not really have, and brought me headaches, life lessons and new skills I did not really want. Also lovely roommates, new neighbors and would-be suitors. Two succeeded: a tree trimmer who returned to his Harley and a termite inspector who returned to his wife.

So, while still looking for my true love of the human variety, I am currently wedded to 1,460 square feet of nuisance and responsibility. It *was* love at first sight.

Sara Alexander is a psychotherapist, writer, artist, and country western dancer currently at home in a 1908 San Francisco Victorian and working towards her next home: a motor home in the Nevada desert.

The ancient Romans thought that by hammering nails on their houses they could nail down or turn aside disease or ill fortune.

Past and Present Pain

 Home can be the most unhappy and dangerous place on earth when you live with an abusive parent. Because that parent worked at home, I could never escape him. Even now the memories don't fade.

I haven't lived there for thirty years, and my father is dead now, but my mother still lives there. Even today, when I round the last curve, a wave of nausea sweeps over me. It is a place where I am always anxious because old memories make me feel unsafe. My mother is disturbed when I begin to tremble and feel ill, and she doesn't understand my feelings now that my father has died and circumstances are different. My childhood home is saturated with painful memories and makes me feel miserable and frightened.

Anonymous

Peace, like charity, begins at home.

Franklin D. Roosevelt

The Season of Truth

This is valuable experience,
lying in bed with the window open
on a cold, late October morning.
My father might not have understood it
but I have written some of my best poems
this way. Sunlight streams across the floor,
reminding me of my room at the back
of the house in Chicago.
It was always cold there,
I liked it. I could scrape my name
in the ice on the window glass with my fingernail.
It was nicest when the sun shone on the snow
not hot enough to melt it,
but that was rare, usually the sky was gray,
and made me want to get away.
Born in Vienna, my father chose Chicago
to die in. Pigeons pecking in gutters,
frozen overcoats at bus stops.
The coast air is clear, I am happy here.
Chicago comes closest late in the afternoon,
when days are short. Winter, rain,
are more real than the rest. In truth,
that is when I am most relaxed and feel best.

Barry Gifford is a
novelist, screenwriter,
and poet. His most recent
works include *Arise and
Walk*, *Night People*, and
Wild at Heart.

49

The "Homelands"

 I am from South Africa, but have lived in the United States as a political exile since 1980. I was born and raised in East London, which is a town on the eastern cape in South Africa. In 1964, when I was seven years old, my family was forcibly moved by the government from the place where I was born, the house that my father and my family owned, to a place called Mdantsane, in what they said was our homeland, about twenty miles away from East London. Our family house was demolished and there was no compensation from the government.

When they moved us, the government made a point of scattering families and neighbors around, breaking up family and friends. Our family, like so many others, was dumped into an area where there were no amenities, no running water, no electricity, no toilets — just left there in these houses—matchbox houses as we called them.

The houses were all the same: brick houses with two doors. The conditions were wretched. We were living in a strange place and had lost our community and friends — the people who supported us for so many years. This was a place of poverty. Since rent was very expensive and few people could afford it, it was not unusual to find sixteen people living in one two-bedroom house. People had to walk long distances to work, long distances to go to school. The crime rate was high, unemployment was a serious problem,

Through my college years, topping that ridge had always given me a great sense of being home, but time had diminished the emotion and I had begun to suspect that home was less a place than an empty page.
Larry McMurtry

all the things associated with abject poverty were there.

It was hard on all of us, but it crushed my father who died about two years after we moved to the Homelands. He struggled to maintain his dignity, but I believe that having our home taken away from us ultimately caused his early death.

Homes in South Africa were not always safe places. Every black South African was issued a passbook, and we were required to carry them at all times. If we were caught without them we could be thrown in jail. Sometimes the police would break into homes in the middle of the night to see our passbooks. That happened to us many times.

My elder brother has a friend who worked for the South African Allied Workers Union, a very militant trade union. He was an inspiration to me and many others. The house where he lived with his mother and his daughter, like others in the "Homelands," had been constructed by the government so that it could be locked from the outside with a padlock. One night the police came to his house and padlocked it, put barriers on the windows, and set the place on fire—hoping my brother's friend was inside. He was not, but his house was destroyed and his elderly mother and five-year-old daughter were killed.

Home is a place where you are supposed to have peace of mind—where you are able to come together with your family. Little did we know that a home can also be a death trap or a burial ground—in this case, a cremation site.

Let us have in our houses, rooms where there shall be space to carry on the business of life freely and with pleasure.

Barry Parker and Raymond Unwin, ***The Art of Building a Home***

Even this tragedy could not make our friend give up the cause of racial justice in South Africa. A week later, while they were burying his daughter and his mother, the police came and opened fire at the funeral. They killed his wife. He was detained and kept in prison for a couple of months. He came out still as uncompromising as he had been from the very beginning.

For the people who lived under such conditions, home could only be a place to go to sleep after working hard all day. We were not safe in our homes, and we had no peace of mind.

I didn't realize how much leaving South Africa meant to me until I had been exiled for many years. It is really difficult to be away from people who mean a lot to you, people with whom you once shared your life.

Now that I live in San Francisco with my American wife, our home is a sacred place to me. I am constantly aware of and thankful for the fact that I have complete control over my home—that no one can enter without my permission and we have a safe home where we can rest and relax. I learn every day what home is all about.

My wife and I are saving money to return to South Africa to visit the friends and family I left behind. I can't wait to go home.

Bongumzi Wowo Busika was born in East London, South Africa, in 1957. He has lived and attended school in Tanzania, Egypt, the former Soviet Union, and the United States. He currently works as a graphic artist with ambitions for the future that include teaching and filmmaking.

It is the place of renewal and of safety, where for a little while there will be no harm or attack and, while every sense is nourished, the soul rests.

May Sarton

Life in the Shelter

 Some women have built nests, filling the small spaces around and on their bunks with personal belongings—pillows, pictures, quilts—belongings they must remove every morning between eight and ten, leaving their cubicles bare or their belongings will be thrown away. Every morning they tear down. Every afternoon they rebuild.

Candace Jane Bacaro has been writing while experiencing the difficulty of being homeless. Her piece was written in a homeless shelter in San Francisco.

The strength of a nation is derived from the integrity of its homes.

Confucius

Homewind Bound

Around Casper, Wyoming, the wind blows more often than not. As James Henley once put it, "the wind is forever on around here." James also renamed the town of Medicine Bow, that lonely stretch where Owen Wister wrote *The Virginian*, "Medicine Blow." The Shoshone sent braves into the Snowy Range near Laramie to seek wind visions. More than one suicide in and around Casper has been attributed to the wind.

Scientifically speaking, the jet stream tends to dip down through Casper, crosses Shirley Rim, a high plateau known for its abundance of rattlesnakes and sage grouse, and sweeps down through Laramie and over the Medicine Bow Range to Cheyenne. Whatever the cause, the wind has left its mark on the people of south-central Wyoming. One could say that it has permanently affected their psyches.

Many never adapt to the wind. Of those who do not, many never move away from it. They stay put as if dug in for a long battle. The most fanatical of this type choose to live in houses perched atop windswept buttes or in colonies of trailer houses set out on the prairie without the protection of trees. I have known many of this type. I have drunk many a bargain beer with them while trying to hear the television over the wind thrashing at aluminum siding and the racket of spouses complaining. The worst thing about trailers and wind is the inevitable draft, the impossibility of stillness, the

Three things are to be looked to in a building: that it stand on the right spot; that it be securely founded; that it be successfully executed.

Goethe

absence of silence. The inhabitants of these trailers are veterans of war. They do not belong there. Yet they stay. Everyone has heard of Vietnam vets yearning for the jungle after returning stateside. Nothing else is sufficient to maintain their skewed interpretations of reality. It is much the same with those who wage war against the wind. They are a tough people. For the most part they are a good people. Their peculiarity is that they choose to live among the enemy.

Although the wind always tests (certain cottonwood and pine trees are forever bent, wheat grass is sometimes in danger of being uprooted, cattle huddle in scraggy hollows in the attempt to ward off the wind's chill brand…), some people choose to view it as an ally. After all, it is the wind that spreads seeds and strengthens roots. Eroded earth finds its way to the alluvial plain or the ocean where, after an expanse of time, it is transformed into new rock. In short, some people view the wind as an agent of rebirth. These people are strong because they surround themselves with allies. It is this type, I believe, who would seek the wind out and ask it for visions.

The name window comes from a cluster of Anglo-Saxon words and means "wind's eye."

In the hope that the strain does not prove too much, I have chosen to stand with the wind rather than against it upon my return home.

John M. Gist was raised in Wyoming. After a bout of wandering, he obtained a B.A. in English at the University of Wyoming. He is now pursuing a M.F.A. in writing at the University of Fairbanks, Alaska, where the wind rarely blows but the vast expanses somehow compensate for it.

They Called Me the Tarzan of Central Park

 I was five when I began climbing, and I climbed anything I could, including rocks, buildings, and lampposts. At eight, I started climbing trees and really found them very challenging; with all the different types of trees there were endless possibilities. Over the years my climbing abilities improved, and I discovered the art of shinnying a tree (like a bear), which enabled me to climb taller and thicker trees. By the time I was thirteen, I enjoyed sitting and relaxing in the tops of tall trees with their amazing views of midtown Manhattan. That is when I decided to build a platform to enable me to sit comfortably while I took in the view and cherished the privacy.

Over the next eight years I built a series of twelve tree houses, one after the other as the Parks Department discovered my houses and destroyed them. It took about an average of three weeks to complete a typical tree house, with each becoming more complex than the one before. My last one (built when I was twenty-one) had five levels and could accommodate ten to fifteen people.

Although the view of the stars at night in New York City was not the best, I still enjoyed gazing at them before going to sleep in my tree houses. It was very relaxing and satisfying to have my

Home Sweet Home.
**John Howard Payne,
1823**

56

own place, safe from all the madness of the city below. I've always loved being in the country and hiking in the remotest woods of upstate New York, and this seemed the next best thing. My mother worried about me when I slept in the park (about four times in any given week), but she knew I was safe because I was up high in the tallest trees which no one else could climb. Even if they could, there would be no reason to do so because they didn't know I was there.

In September 1985, the Parks Department and the Central Park Conservancy caught me in my last tree house. They woke me up in the morning while they were attempting to tear down the house. I offered to assist them, and they were so impressed by my free-hand tree-climbing abilities that they offered me a job, which I gladly accepted. I worked in the park for four years taking care of the trees before I quit to form my own arboriculture business.

I still enjoy climbing trees when I work, and I know that deep-down I want to build more tree houses, because up there I truly feel at home.

Bob Redman lives in an apartment in New York City's Upper West Side. In 1989 he left the Central Park Conservancy to form his own business called Redman Tree Experts. Currently, an independent film company is planning a documentary on his tree house building exploits. Someday he plans to build another tree house.

A Piece of the Rock

 A houseboat is not a piece of the rock. It's not even stationary. I can count on getting seasick in my own living room several times a year. My chandelier kisses the ceiling, paintings clatter on the walls, and ropes strain to keep my home from going south the hard way. God forbid it should develop a leak.

So you see that a sense of security could be a problem on a houseboat.

So could quiet.

With every sunrise that spreads behind the masts in the harbor, the freshening breeze strums the rigging like Hurricane Andrew.

The hulk of an ancient ferry rests nearby, rotting and gray but not at peace, its spine breaking with a terrifying snap every so often. Courting grebes run insanely on the surface of the water, while great blue herons screech. Humming toadfish haunt our nights with their mating song—a reverberating hum that sounds like a transformer about to explode and was a major problem for PG&E until a marine biologist discovered their dirty little secret. At Christmas, barking sea lions and dive-bombing pelicans compete in a brutal frenzy for herring, and only the most fortified kayakers venture out to go caroling after dark.

Privacy? Forget it. My neighbors have no shame and no clothes by the looks of them. At any hour, they stroll into my living room in their robes with empty coffee cups to borrow a guitar string. Perfect strangers with flowing red hair and a sack of organic artichokes row by to discuss fractals and invite you to cook for them. Olympic athletes bathe naked by moon or sun.

If it's privacy you're after, you'd be better off at the airport.

Sure. I was warned about all these problems. My ex-accountant who works in a mall and lives in a townhouse development urged me to buy a condo where I could gain some equity. A nice little piece of real estate in a suburban cul-de-sac where people have last names and decent TV reception. A houseboat is nothing but a dream wrapped in fog and suspended between the mud and stars. You'll never be able to sell it, he said.

Profit. That could be another problem.

Boredom, on the other hand, is never a problem.

Home is the place to do the things you want to do. Here we eat just when we want to. Breakfast and luncheon are extremely moveable feasts. It's terrible to allow conventional habits to gain a hold on a whole household; to eat, sleep and live by clock ticks.

Zelda Fitzgerald

A writer and artist, **Cynthia Franco** has traveled around the world as a photo-journalist, scrambled up mountains in the Himalayas, crewed on a tall ship, and assisted in whale rescues. She aspires to stay home in Sausalito, California.

Home, Away From Home

 Comparisons, as they say, are odious. But you never stop comparing.

You live in the same place for half of your life, reach an alleged age of reason, and move away forever from all that you know toward something you only suspect you might be. Over the years you go back, but not really. Because, as the original Tom Wolfe pointed out, you can't do that. And you wouldn't want to anyway. You left after all (and stayed away) for bigger, better, and brighter lights—of the intellectual as well as the electrical persuasion.

Except lately…the lights don't seem to dazzle as they used to. Maybe you've been staring straight into them for too long. Maybe you just don't like what they illuminate these days.

You find yourself wondering about the future and wandering over the past. You go back where you started and you compare.

It's simpler here, you think. It's quieter and neater and the sidewalk doesn't smell like a toilet. Even on half of your salary you could afford to buy a house.

At dusk, when the temperature drops below 90, you run silently through the same suburban streets that you walked and biked and thought of as wide when you were a child. As they did thirty years ago, the streets eventually dissolve into an unkempt field,

*Surely it's better
to live in the country,
to live on a prairie by
a drawing of rivers,
in Iowa or Illinois or
Indiana, say, than
in any city, in any
stinking fog of human
beings, in any
blooming orchard
of machines.
It ought to be.*
William Gass

bordered by railroad tracks and thick with Queen Anne's lace, milkweed pods, and tall rustling grass.

Cicadas are your Walkman, lightening bugs, wild rabbits, and swooping bats your only company. The silent rails gleam dully in the dying light and run west toward the setting sun. West toward the four rented rooms on the edge of the Pacific that you now call home.

For two whole weeks, you realize, you have not been treated to the sight of a mother and child huddled in a doorway. That, you must admit, has done more to restore your appetite for life than anything else on this vacation.

Yet you know there are poor here. They slump in line at the supermarket with their food stamps, hold handwritten signs asking for work outside the town mall. They line up by the score at the Catholic soup kitchen where your mother volunteers.

Poverty isn't absent, only less conspicuous than in the big city. Children here get killed, abused, neglected, and lied to; you just find out about it in the morning paper. There is drug addiction, alcoholism, bulimia, AIDS, psychosis, moral corruption, and free-floating anxiety too.

The numbers can't match the big city's, but the proportions do.

When you look past the surface, past your own uneasy present and your irretrievable past, what you see here is what you see everywhere. Not bliss. Not peace. Just the human condition:

A man travels the world over in search of what he needs and returns home to find it.

George Moore

61

people struggling to be happy (or at least not unhappy) and trying hard to do the right thing—whatever that is.

You think of your good friend in Italy, the place you consider paradise on earth. He is sick of it, says his last letter, sick of nothing working, sick of the unions, sick of the comedia dell'Arte that is his country's government. You see Italy only on vacation, he reminds you. Living here is different. Living here, Switzerland looks better every day.

It is always a trade off, isn't it? City life, small-town life, Italy, Switzerland, life on a prairie by a drawing of rivers. There is no "better," only what works 51 percent of the time. For you.

Return to your roots. It sounds so right, especially when the roots run deep and wide and the part of the plant that is above ground looks like hell.

But home is where the heart is, even if it's only a half-hearted heart. Your heart is not in your roots and hasn't been for ages. For a thousand reasons it is on the edge of the Pacific, in four rented rooms where you keep your keys and a canister of Mace by the door.

It isn't easy, it isn't quiet, it isn't neat. It is, however, home.

Stephanie Salter has been a writer for the *San Francisco Examiner* since 1976 and an opinion columnist since 1987. She is the author of *The Home of The Brave: Profiles in Words and Pictures of Bay Area Homeless Families* and a contributing essayist in Ron Fimrite's baseball collection, *Birth of a Fan*.

Building

 I like building houses. There's something very satisfying about working with your hands and making something, changing or improving something. I particularly like being able to take somebody's dream about what they would like to see in their house and make it into a reality.

I've spent a lot of time in the last twenty years remodeling, helping people to change their home into what they want or to increase its value. A house is simply a shell or a shelter from the elements, and the difference between a house and a home is how it is personalized and how people's personalities shape the environment to make it compatible with them.

The analogy that comes to my mind is birds when they look for a place to build a nest. Different kinds of birds will pick different types of trees or bushes or poles because of what they are and what they need. I think people are the same way. Different people look for different houses to build their nests in because they have different needs. It's a matter of understanding what you're about and what you need to make your nest happen.

Eric Angress grew up on a farm in Marin County, California, where he became accustomed to working outside and with his hands. Now a contractor, he works with many different clients to shape their houses into spaces they call home.

Home, the idea of home, is my principal purpose. If people have bought a house as an investment or chosen the furniture because they'll be able to sell it for more, you can tell in two minutes. You know, our parents didn't buy a house as an investment. They bought it as a place to bring you up, to give you roots.

Sister Parish

How to Make a House a Home

- Banish all overhead lights (the ones up in the ceiling). Favor lamps with translucent shades, especially in the kitchen, next to the stove, and on the kitchen table. Don't use anything higher than a 25-watt bulb; 7 1/2-watt appliance bulbs are even better.

- Buy three clay pots and saucers and plant three red geraniums in the pots. Line them up in a sunny windowsill.

- Procure the best all-cotton sheets you can afford—white only. Send them out to be laundered and pressed. Once a week you'll be rewarded when you slip inside a smooth, cotton envelope, ready to seal your dreams.

- Find an old bird cage and buy a canary that really sings. Hang the bird cage from the ceiling in a bright room, preferably one in which you spend time in the morning. Hang a fancy tassel from the bottom of the bird cage.

- Put a toaster on your breakfast table.

- Hang a bird feeder outside the window next to the table where you eat breakfast. Keep a bird identification book at the table. Learn the names of the friends you eat breakfast with.

- Cook a stew, light a fire in the fireplace, and invite a friend over for dinner at the last minute.

- Put your favorite art in your bathroom where you can enjoy it up close and intimately.

- Light at least one candle each evening before you begin preparing dinner. Be thankful for what you have.

- Paint your dining room warm red. Put black paper shades on all the lamps and little ones on the chandelier.

- Buy expensive wood polish—one that smells the way wood polish should smell—and polish your tables once a week.

- Find really good thick bath mats. When you step out of a shower or bath, it's great to have something to cuddle your toes into.

- Keep the things that mean something to you—granite stones from a beach in Maine, a bird's nest that fell from a tree, a pine cone, your nephew's watercolors—close at hand where they can be enjoyed. Don't worry if they're not in the best of taste.

- A home can't have too many books.

- Find an old wine glass that you really like and keep it just for yourself.

- Treat your family like guests and your guests like family.

Native to California's Napa Valley, **A. Cort Sinnes** is the author of more than twenty books on gardening, outdoor living, and grill cooking. His syndicated newspaper column, "In Your Own Backyard," appears in more than 250 newspapers nationwide.

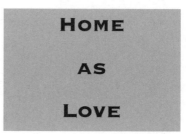

HOME

AS

LOVE

Some luck lies in not getting what
you thought you wanted but getting what you
have, which once you have it you may be smart enough to
see is what you would have wanted had you known. He takes deep
breaths and the cold air goes to his brain and makes him more
sensible. He starts out on the short walk to the house where
people love him and will be happy to see his face.

Garrison Keillor,
Lake Wobegone Days

My Home is a Rainbow

"Home is somewhere to store the heart…because home is one
  mind with no frayed ends, a place to be yourself, a place to hide
  from everything but love…."

Ellie Cella, age nine

"Home makes me think of the good parts of life if I have had a
  bad day. Home makes me feel safe, it makes me feel wanted and
  cared for. Home makes me feel settled and comfortable. Home
  makes me feel cool. Home makes me feel good."

Holmes Futrell, age eight

"Home is a place to be loved. It can be fun and it can be not fun.
  Home is where my pets are. Home is a place to love other people.
  Home is where my dreams are. Home is where I feel safe."

Geraldine Chavez Bourne, age eight

"Home can mean a yelling screaming teenager or a loving mom
  and dad who will cheer me up when I am feeling down.
  Sometimes messy, sometimes clean."

Hannah Lesser, age eight

"Home is where you live. It's where you go after school. I like my home. It's warm and snug. My brother drives me crazy. He can be annoying. At other times I like to wrestle with him. Sometimes I read to my mom and dad and sometimes they read to me."

Brian Zimmerman, age eight

"My house is a house of fun and laughter, but also of work and hardship. We work hard on the ranch, trying to keep everything alive. It is a place where you know you are always wanted. It is a place where you should stay till you think you can face the world by yourself and support your family and yourself."

Tom Reich, age twelve

"My home is a rainbow leading to happiness. It isn't the furniture, the cozy and warm furniture, the rooms so peaceful and quiet, but the people who are in it that cast a shadow of love over me."

Adina Fleming, age eight

A Tiny Russian Village

 Ever since I can remember, I felt connected to my Russian grandmother. She was uneducated, nearly illiterate, and she spoke with a thick, Yiddish accent. She lived in Brooklyn; she had a circumscribed life that included little more than shopping, cooking, cleaning, and going to the synagogue, and she had the softest skin I have ever touched. She came from a small shtetl in Russia, and her life there had been so restricted that she didn't even know *where* in Russia it was located. With prodding, she was able to tell me the name of a nearby town. I pored over maps of Russia, but the town was so small I couldn't locate it. "Grandma, please, tell me the name of a nearby city." She shrugged. "Gram, I need to know where, exactly, you come from." She paused a moment. "I come from far. That's where I come from." In Russia there had been poverty and pogroms; she did everything she could to forget it.

I left the USA and went to live in Europe and North Africa for most of my adult life. Strangely, the more time I spent away from my grandmother, the more I became convinced that I was connected to her. I wanted to know more about her shtetl; somehow I felt that it was my shtetl too. I spoke about it endlessly in

Europe. My friends teased me and said it was my obsession. They gave me a nickname: the name of the shtetl.

Once, when I was riding a train outside of Paris I began to chat with an older man, and he told me that he was from Russia. I asked him if he knew my grandmother's village. "Yes, yes," he said with obvious excitement. Then he looked out the window— it was his stop. He got off the train, apologizing that he couldn't tell me more about the tiny village.

I decided that I had to prod my grandmother. She was getting older. What if she passed away, and I could never find out?

I was terrified to fly, and so I took a ship back to the USA and went to see my grandmother. Her soft skin had wrinkled considerably, her glasses were thicker, and her feet were swollen. I ate some of her boiled chicken, hugged her dearly, and then began to interview her. I pulled out a small white pad and asked her to tell me everything she knew about the shtetl.

She stared at me quizzically. Why would I be interested in such things? I got very specific. I asked her what fruits and vegetables she ate and what she wore to market. I found out that she envied the non-Jewish girls in their uniforms, because they went to school and she was not allowed to study. I found out that the floor of her house was made of goat manure and that she worked long hours

America was where all my mother's hopes lay. She had come here in 1949 after losing everything in China: her mother and father, her family home, her first husband and two daughters, twin baby girls. But she never looked back with regret. There were so many ways for things to get better.

Amy Tan,
The Joy Luck Club

71

in the fields as a child picking tobacco leaves. "Feh, feh, feh," she said. "This is silly." But to me it wasn't silly; it was vital, riveting information.

When I returned to Europe, I wrote a play about the village. In French. A Swiss audience came to see the play. Maybe they wondered why in the world I was writing about such things. Why would a very contemporary American woman be obsessed by the early 1900s in a Russian shtetl?

After ten years in Europe, I returned to the USA and I ended up in Los Angeles with my first job in Hollywood. I knew no one. My younger sister gave me the name of a man who was a friend of a friend. At least I could call and say hello.

I called, and he came to meet me. It was like meeting my other half. We agreed about everything, had every taste in common, and laughed ourselves sick on our first date. We saw each other seven or eight times, and then he invited me to meet his parents.

The big meeting took place in a Chinese restaurant. I sat down and saw his folks scrutinizing me. I tried to make chitchat and to find some common ground. I asked them where they were born, and they said they were both born in America. "Oh," I said, wanting to show interest. "And where are your parents from?" His father smiled and said, "From a tiny little town in Russia. I'm sure you never heard of it." And then it happened. He spoke the

There should be at least a room or some corner where no one will find you and disturb you or notice you.
Thomas Merton

name of my grandmother's shtetl. We were from the same village!

I consulted a famous rabbi, and he said he had never heard of such a thing. Two Americans whose grandparents came from the same minuscule shtetl, meet and fall in love. It was a great coincidence, and it must be a great blessing!

Two years later, we were married. For part of the ceremony we used a spoon that my husband's father found in a drawer; it was the sole remnant he had of life in that shtetl.

My husband and I have since traveled extensively and lived in many places. Sometimes I feel a little disoriented; I don't know where "home" is. When this happens, I turn to my husband and ask him, "Where is home?" He smiles at me, and I smile back at him.

We both know where our home is, although I have still never found it on a map.

Germanic people associated the call of the cuckoo with good fortune, and that is why the cuckoo comes out of a clock to call the hours and wish prosperity day after day.

Judith Fein is an award-winning screenwriter, playwright, and opera librettist, and claims that's all she knows how to do in life. Her first book, *Indian Time*, was published in 1993. She lives in Santa Fe, New Mexico, with her husband, who knows how to do everything.

A Haunted House

 The first home my husband and I bought was haunted. It had been built by a wealthy man for his wife, Emily, who died of a brain tumor in the house.

After we moved in we got to know Emily intimately. She was a benign spirit, but she insisted on making her presence known in peculiar ways.

The first night we slept there, my husband and I heard a knock on our bedroom door in the middle of the night. It was our son, sleeping bag in hand, asking to sleep in our room. "Emily is driving me nuts," he said. "She's been banging on the pipes all night."

I woke up another morning at six o'clock and it sounded as if all of the toilets and faucets were running at the same time. I got up, checked the whole house inside and out, and found no water running. When I wearily asked Emily to please be quiet and let us sleep, the sound of rushing water stopped.

Sometimes things disappeared, never to be found again. One day I was sorting snapshots at our dining room table. I left the room to answer the phone and when I returned just minutes later one of the three piles of photos was missing. We never found them—not even after major remodeling work or after we moved.

The modern idea of home has been well expressed as the place one goes from the garage.

George Wickersham

Despite her antics, we became very fond of Emily. But one winter morning, she did something that endeared her to us forever. Our son was asleep in his bedroom in the basement when he was awakened by Emily banging on the pipes. Even though she usually stopped when asked, this time she kept banging and banging. When he finally opened his eyes, the room was filled with smoke. The furnace was on fire. He fell to the floor and crawled out of the room to safety.

Sometime after the fire, a friend gave us an old photograph of Emily. We kept it in the living room, and as we passed it we would thank her for saving our son. We would also tell her she was welcome in the home but always free to go. Emily continued to live with us for several more years, but she visited us less and less frequently. I think her spirit was finally released from the house.

Sue Patton Thoele and her husband conceived and constructed their current home in Boulder, Colorado, around the word "sanctuary." She is a writer and psychotherapist who has written four books, including *The Woman's Book of Courage* and *The Courage to be Yourself.*

From ghoulies and ghosties and long leggety beasties And things that go bump in the night Good Lord, deliver us!
Scottish Prayer

The Garden

 I didn't know when I gave Miggs a start of violets from my garden that they would spread across her flagstone patio or that one day she would give me a start back for my new garden.

I didn't know when I separated from my husband that I would never walk in my garden again, never pick a rose or have tea in the morning and watch the spiders.

I loved my house, but it was the garden that made it home, and it was the garden that was the hardest to leave. It was three years before I had a garden again, an ugly bare patch around a new suburban house. And my friends came, all with bits of my garden that I had shared with them. One gave me back the pale gray iris that flowers so early and is so fragrant. One gave me the rose geranium whose leaves keep the linen closet so sweet. And Miggs brought me Parma violets.

Every week there is a new bloom in my garden, and the memory of the friend who brought me a piece of my garden again.

Jill Appenzeller, a former corporate executive turned landscape architect, designs small side gardens in cramped urban settings or creates landscape plans for large estate gardens. Her landscape business is based in Danville, California.

Open Arms

 It's always good to be home where they let me draw on the walls or bounce my ball down the hall 'cause it's my home too. That was thirty years ago—today home is anywhere I am that I get to be me. Where I can never laugh too loud, or sleep too late. Where I can stay up until tomorrow like I did last night because I'm home.

If I leave home I can return as champion or penniless prodigal and the same open arms welcome and hold me for as long as I am there.

Like last night, when I stayed up all night drawing on the walls. But I'm older now, so it looked more like painting the bedroom. Home is where I go when I can't go anywhere else.

Craig McNair Wilson is a writer, director, and creativity teacher to corporate America. He owns a craftsman-style house in the heart of "Bungalow Heaven," a historic landmark district in Pasadena, California. There's a lone redwood tree in his front yard and mother and daughter daschunds (they came with the house) in the backyard. Between the two is home.

Generations upon Generations

 My home is my refuge from the outside world, a place of calm where there are no loud voices and no need to act or to react. Maybe that is why I hate listening to rock or pop music at home, a habit that my friends find bizarre (some bring their own music when they come for dinner).

But my liking for serenity at home is very American, a tendency that I probably picked up from having lived here for so many years. In Hong Kong, where I grew up, people feel uncomfortable unless they are surrounded by chattering family and friends. Activities are done en masse. Cars are crammed to capacity for outings and it is rare to dine out with less than eight to ten. A wealthy friend of our family even travels around the world with an entourage of at least twenty friends, visiting hotel upon hotel that he owns.

The Chinese feel comfortable in crowds because their homes are also noisy and bustling. Up to four generations can live together under one roof—the more the merrier. My parents were educated in the United States, so our "Westernized" family lived separately. But we still observed family rituals, one of which was Sunday family dinners at my *maa maa's* (my father's mother).

It was always loud and crowded on Sundays at *maa maa's*. She had seventeen children and even more grandchildren, and

Home is not where you live but where they understand you.

Christian Morgenstern

second and third cousins would be there too. By the time we arrived, usually about an hour before the meal, the rest of the family would have already been there all afternoon, gossiping, playing, and eating. There would be familiar faces in every room, and at least six people squished into the sofa in the living room. Even with so many people there *maa maa* would always see us arrive and come to greet us with her own butter cookies and, my favorite, homemade caramelized walnuts with dried figs.

I still dream of those figs and walnuts and *maa maa's* cooking. Dinner was served family style, with large platters of beef, pork, poultry, fish and other seafood, and several vegetables placed on a lazy Susan on the table. Everyone helped themselves, taking bite-sized portions from the platters. The children were given a little from each platter on a small plate to keep them from eating only their favorite dish or spinning the lazy susan faster and faster and out of control.

When our family immigrated to the United States, those dinners were among the things I missed most. Years later, when *maa maa* passed away one night quietly in her sleep, I thought of the comfort of her crowded home and simple dishes. Perhaps I will also have a home where many generations come to share Sunday dinners.

Born and raised in Hong Kong, **Agnes Ng** now lives in the San Francisco Bay Area. She works as a publicist "around the clock" and, in her spare time, is starting a family of her own.

One must remember that there is a difference between a house, a place of shelter, and a home, a place where all your affections are centered.
Lucy Maynard Simon,
The Domestic Service,
Prisoners of Poverty,
1897

Happy to be Home

 My partner and I decided to make a quick pilgrimage to New York City for a few days of museums and bright lights and all those foods not to be found in our corner of rural New Mexico. I haven't been to New York in over a decade, and I often think I'm missing a lot living in a place where the nearest weekly newspaper is forty miles down the road (and it's seventy miles to a daily). The airfare has hit a five-year low, our ex-New Yorker friends are going too; we have a Manhattan apartment to house-sit—what could be better? The night before our departure the chestnut mare colics—a simple intestinal cramp that can be fatal for horses—and we cancel our trip.

By the next morning, as the plane leaves Albuquerque with our friends and without us, the mare is recovering in the nonchalant manner of horses, impatient for breakfast, brushing off the careful attention she welcomed the night before. All day I'm at the edge of tears as I water the garden, clean the house, wash the saddle blankets out front in the wheelbarrow. I'm disappointed, but that feeling is like shrugging a fly off my shoulder. The hidden tears are something bigger, some feeling more solemn and grand and hard to name. All day I look for words, but all I can say, finally, is how happy I am to be home.

Gina Covina is a writer and artist living in New Mexico. She has recently converted an old barn into her adobe home.

The View

 Up ahead. There, where the laundry is drying on the line in the yard. Where the brick path and the wooden shutters and the big rooms are all lit up. Where the man inside is at the sink, washing lettuce and tomatoes and carrots, cutting the onions into thin purple strips, and the woman in the next room is lifting the baby into the air.

And as the man prepares the pan where he will cook the dinner, he walks from the sink to the stove, humming tunes from big band songs. And the woman laughs as she watches the baby point at the night that has begun to fall outside, where there is ivy and hydrangea and a row of pine trees at the edge of the woods, where tiny stars float above the stream. And after dinner the man asks the woman to dance while the baby looks around and laughs about everything she cannot yet say.

Later, when the candles flicker and the man and the woman sit in the living room, they look out their wide window toward the view they can no longer see. The man puts his arms around the woman, and when they talk, they talk about the hills that surround their home. Their parents. The children they used to be. Maybe they talk about the future. Maybe they sit, holding hands, and dream about the baby as the laundry hangs on the long white line.

Last August, **Karen Benke** completed her M.A. in writing and is currently finishing her first novel. She lives in Marin County, California.

Feel It and Mend

 When I was a little girl, I spent a lot of time in the hospital—years of weekly visits and twelve surgeries to correct a problem with my eyes—and during this time my relationship with this "home away from home" was firmly, if grudgingly, established.

Hospitals are notoriously scary places for a child, and the mere suggestion of another impending stay inside the walls of this red brick giant reduced me to tears in fearful anticipation of yet more poking and prodding, monster needles, the foul taste of ether, and long nights away from my parents. It was only years later that my memories of those times came back to me tinged with nostalgia— even with a hint of homesickness—that I began to consider what home really means.

Memories of another home visit me. Nights passed in protected slumber on crisp, starched sheets. Cool, antiseptic air, and the light, brisk footsteps of nurses peeking in on patients, appearing at bedsides to check temperature and pulse. Fruit ice served in a cup, soothing sweetness at midnight.

Now I see the hospital as a home where comfort cannot be promised, but where caring and acceptance are freely given. Where you are loved and your pain is shared, even when all anyone can do is hold your hand and cry along with you. Where you can be the hero, or you can whimper and sob without losing face. It's a place to lick your wounds, to come when you're broken and stay until you're whole. Where you mend when life breaks you, where you rest and take your medicine and find your spirit and strength renewed.

"Leave me alone!" I remember demanding, angry about the still more pills I was expected to swallow or the application of a new, scratchy dressing under my eye patch. I remember pulling the stiff covers up over my head until I heard the nurse's slippers padding softly away. An hour later she returned, rebuffs forgiven, answering my plaintive "I'm thirsty" with a cup of apple juice and an extra blanket. Gentle reassurance in the night.

Stop a clock at the hour of death or bad luck will stay in the house.

Sometimes when I can't sleep, when the stillness outside my apartment window matches the silence between the walls, a light left burning in the hall makes me feel less alone, as though someone might poke their head in to check on me now and then. And on these nights when the day comes back to me, and events roll over upon each other in my brain—arguments, disappointments, a critical remark, an opportunity missed, friendships neglected— I get up and pour a cup of apple juice, find another blanket in the closet, and cradle myself as thoughts invite me to feel the pain again. To feel it and mend.

Andrea K. Orrill is a journalist in her hometown of Saratoga, New York. She is currently finishing a book about eating disorders.

The Joy of Being at Home

 The Hamburger Helper is sending disagreeable odors though the house. The dogs are playing in the entryway, and one is eating the toe of my leather moccasin. My husband tramps up and down the carpeted stairs with his snow-covered tough-enough-for-Minnesota macho boots. One child has left half-finished artwork on nearly every flat surface and is making yet another sugar-laden cake. The other child is practicing her tap dancing on the cement laundry room floor, and the staccato sound makes my cheekbones hurt. The cat keeps rolling over and stretching—her sign for "give me attention *now*." The water softener needs salt, the couch sags with age, the dryer is buzzing, and there are nose prints on both sides of the deck door.

I love it all. It makes me laugh and revel in the joy of being in the safe serenity of my home.

Cheryl Erickson is an educator and homemaker. She and her family make their home near Minneapolis, Minnesota.

Moving On

 For thirty years I woke up in my home town: Boulder, Colorado. I went to sleep every night nestled at the foot of the Rocky Mountains. Three magnificent slabs of granite—the Flatirons—were my touchstones. I watched the sun set behind them through the story of my life—they were my bookmarks. The seasons changed and so did I, but they never did. If I went away, even for a day, I knew as I crested the last hill on the way into town that they would be waiting for me, holding my place.

Then, one day, I fell in love. I was a thousand miles away from the foothills of Colorado, in the San Francisco International Airport. On a moving walkway, looking into the eyes of the woman who would be my wife. I realized that this was my home. I got on a plane and left without telling her. I had to see the Flatirons one more time to make sure. They were still there, but I had moved on. I called her that night to tell her. My home was with her, in the mountains, by the sea, in the trees, in her heart.

David Caven's family built a cabin in the mountains as a summer home when he was a child. When he feels homesick now, what he misses are the rocks, the pines, the view, the wood stove, and the outhouse.

The Soft Hum of Love

 I live at the edge of the wilderness, in a house as old as the trees that shade it. My window looks out to the mountain that bears my small daughter's name. I hear her playing downstairs, squealing with delight as she chases the dog around the couch. I hear music drifting up and the sound of my husband typing in the next room. If I listen carefully I can hear the water boiling in the pot on the wood stove and the chickadees at the feeder. And if I listen with even more care I can hear the soft hum of love—for this place and for each other, like the sound of a treadle moving needle over cloth, binding it.

Sue Halpern lives in a house at the edge of the Adirondack Park wilderness, with the nearest store fifteen miles away. Her first book is called *Migrations to Solitude*.

I Am

 Our house was built in 1836, a lovely old Vermont farmhouse with huge exposed beams that are even older than the house itself (they probably came from a local barn that collapsed in the early 1800s). Our joke is that it will only take another 150 years to get the house finished to our liking, but it's actually great as it is: slightly funky, but very livable, warm in the winter, cool in the summer, and nestled in acres of meadow and forest. It's my house, but not really my home.

When I reflect on my true home I think of the words "I am." The sense of "I am" is the first thing we realize when we are born and the last thing we still know before we die. I also think the sense of "I am" is perhaps the most direct route to a consciousness greater than ourselves, which includes us, our "I am" sense, and everything else. Many people would call this all-encompassing consciousness by the name "God"—I do, too. And I believe that this sense of "I am" outlasts the body, outlasts the personality, outlasts the individual mind that we all prize so highly during this lifetime. And so, like my house, my body/mind personality, much as I enjoy living in it, is not my home. "I am" is my home. God is my home.

David Harp has over twenty-four books in print, including *The Three Minute Meditator*. After seventeen years in San Francisco he recently pulled up roots and moved with his family to Vermont.

A Home in Dresden

 I grew up in a home my father built in Dresden, Germany. There were beds of roses, a pond for my toy boat, beautiful chandeliers, silver tea sets, and expensive tapestries. In 1938, the Nazis forced my father to sell the house and confiscated the money. He died in a concentration camp. My mother committed suicide. I escaped to London and then to America with Lore, my wife.

In German they have the word *heimat* which means "native place." That's one facet of home, there is no doubt, but the place where you were born or raised isn't necessarily where you want to be. For me, home is not where I come from. I've lived in America over fifty-five years, much longer than in Germany, and served in the American army in the Pacific theatre of war during World War II. Germany is definitely not home—I wouldn't think of going back to live there. There are no more memories left there for me. Everything was torn out. America is my country.

Sixteen years ago I began the long process of reclaiming my family home from the German government. I wrote letters and made three trips back to Germany. Our beautiful house had been sold, and under the East German government it was turned into a student residence for the university. It wasn't until the third visit that I was even allowed to step inside the house.

Where thou art, that, is home.

Emily Dickinson

When I first entered I closed my eyes and knew exactly how I felt when I was living there. But so much had changed since my family and I lived there that the memories faded fast. Walls had been moved, and the garden and surrounding grounds had been donated to a Lutheran church, which used it to rebuild a church that was destroyed during the war. It was no longer our family home. After sixteen years of phone calls, letters, and paperwork, I got our family home back, but still haven't received the land where the Lutheran church now stands.

Home is the place where, when you have to go there, they have to take you in.

Robert Frost

But I still don't consider it my home. Homes of wood and brick and plaster are only temporary. As I found out, people can be easily uprooted. But wherever you are, you can have a home. As long as you live, you have something in mind that is your home. Home is something you make, you yourself make it. And the people who cannot make a home for themselves are forever vacillating and are unhappy. Home is where you feel secure. And even if you live under persecution, home is still where you feel secure. Home is where you belong. Home is where they expect you.

In my case, home is where Lore, my wife of fifty-six years, is.

Hans Shaper lives with his wife and their Chesapeake retriever in Point Richmond, California. They have two adult children. Hans has retired from his business to work for peace, good will, and international understanding through the scholarship program of the Rotary Foundation of Rotary International.

Finally Home

 As youngsters on the Dakota plains, my brother Floyd and I went to a rural school, either on horseback or in a cart drawn by a gentle, old horse. A horse is an amazing animal. It has an instinct for home and will return to the place where it has lived as a colt no matter how far away.

Once, around 1910 or so, our country class of seven was isolated by a four-day blizzard. We were without food, of course, and out of heat. All the firewood had been burned during the first day and night, and then our wood desks, and the blizzard raged on. Desperate for fuel, a student pulled up a wood board from the floor, and a wild sixty-degree-below-zero wind roared up from below. Soon we would be freezing to death.

Floyd found his way to his old horse, and bridled it. He would ride without a saddle, and the heat of the horse would keep him from freezing while he rode. He roped its neck with his picket-rope, and the seven of us, six students and our teacher, were roped one behind the other to set out through a blizzard so blinding we literally could not see the person directly behind or in front of us. We waded on through knee-deep snow, with Floyd on his old horse leading us, for four miles, five miles, and finally home.

The lucky horseshoe is a throwback to a time when it was thought that witches rode on broomsticks because they were afraid of horses. Nailing a horseshoe over your doorway kept witches from entering.

Floyd's feet were frozen. Mother thawed them slowly in melting snow, and fed us. Dad helped blanket us to sleep on the carpeted floor of the living room. We had no telephone, and neither did our neighbors. If the blizzard quieted, other frantic but helpless parents would go to the school, read the teacher's note on her desk, and then happily drive on to our house to pick up their children.

Winfred Kay Thackrey was born May 15, 1899, in Bismarck, North Dakota. She and her husband have traveled all over the world. Now living in Santa Barbara, California, she is currently shopping for a houseboat to live on.

Flufferbelly

 I am almost fifty years old, and the word "home" only conjures up visions of a small child, evening air alive with the smell of new-mown hay, and a white house with shutters green with paint that today would be almost forty-three years old.

Home. I like the concept of onomatopoeia, of words like "sizzle" whose very sound suggests the meaning of the word itself, but I don't know if there is a term for a word that in itself drags along the weight of memory. Home is such a word. Home.

I have lived in a three-bedroom, two-bath house for twenty-three years. I came with a husband and a baby boy (joined soon by another), and now I leave by myself. The walls are newly painted—Flufferbelly, a warm golden peach tone—and waiting for a new owner. Clean fresh paint covers splatted words of anger, salt tracks of tears, new puppy puddles, baby spills, teenage wrath and agony, beer parties held when parents were absent, and then the illness. Sentimentality aside, home really is the place of private pain and stabbing anger, rawly exposed to those who are skin to skin, blood of blood.

There were joyous times too, but I think those quiver in the air, like motes in the sunshine. First steps and first smiles, slamming the front door and yelling about making the baseball team, birthday and graduation parties, as well as quiet meals eaten with the hungry desperation and silent appreciation of the young. These memories dance like glass shadows thrown by clear windows.

I know a friend who is a realtor, and she says that houses are infected by their owners. Bad owners leave an unhappy house, and she has to work hard to break the cycle. She looks for particularly happy people to move in after an unhappy person has trashed the house and undermined its character.

I hope my house will feel like a home to the next owner. It never has to me, although I tried for years to make it mine. I moved furniture, I painted the walls, I planted a garden, and still it is not my home, and I really don't know why. I am off to the country to try and find that space where the small child smells the fragrance of new-mown hay.

Mimi Luebbermann lives, writes, and gardens in St. Helena, California. She is temporarily living in a converted chicken coop after selling the family home she lived in for twenty-three years. She spends the weekends searching the countryside for the farm of her dreams.

A house full of people is a house full of different points of view.
Maori proverb

93

Mamitá

A canoe. A river in the jungles of Nicaragua. My mother sitting dead center, back erect, child in arms, terrified eyes forward. Two Sumo Indians, one in front guiding with his spear. The other in the rear, eyes roving, aware of every sound and listening for the silence. It is in silence—in the stillness of the animal's voices that death comes. Death: a home we know so well. Perhaps my father is at this home now. We don't know. The soldiers were in the front of the house and we were in the back. Quickly someone grabbed Dona Maria, my "Mamitá," and she grabbed me and she almost fainted several times as she ran from her husband and the nightmare that was theirs, toward the place of unfathomable fears—the swamp. The swamp of all nightmares. The nightmare that would now be ours, just Mamitá's and mine. And yet, it was our salvation, our only hope. Should I insult her by calling her brave? I could not. I can only tell you how it was. This home she created for us.

Lyly Rojas De Knaus lives part of the year in Indonesia doing research with her husband, a University of Vienna ethnologist. She has published *Las Danzas de Mexico*, among other works. Her father escaped death, but later was imprisoned and forced to endure a mock execution by a firing squad. Both he and her mother now live peacefully in the United States.

Root, Leaf, and Flower

For my cousin
Catherine Louise Rudroff
(1958-1984)

Mostly what we come home for now
is to bury the dead,
to walk, as we did as children,
among the stones that bear on their faces
the names we carry in our bones.

In those days it was always summer,
always Sunday, when Grandmother
and her older sister, Agnes,
would gather the children together
to ask which of us would like to go
with them to the cemetery. Even then,
even as children, we knew the ritual
of tending graves.

The stones are clustered in a field
of deepest green like the heavy blossoms of gardenias
weathering in the sun. Grandmother and Aggie
in their crisp starched summer dresses
kneel in the grass beside each grave.
With lopping shears and edger, trowel and spade,

they clip back the weeds, deepen the groove
where the earth ends and the stone begins.

As they work, they say the name half whispered,
and from the name unfold the petals of each life:
their mother, Annie Laura,
their grandmother, Mercy Jane.
Most we never knew, some only briefly;
yet their lives are carved now into memory
as their names are carved into stone.

Just as we are leaving Aggie goes back once more,
cocks the handle of her rusty shears to form a knife
and scrapes out the moss that has begun to grow
in the empty space of each letter, peels back
the soft green gauze that covers the wound,
scraping each name back to the sharp edge of stone.

Cedar, oak, magnolia: all afternoon
their shadows move among us
as we move among the stones.
How deep the roots are buried here,
deeper even than the bones.

• • •

Deep into summer the magnolia blooms,
huge petals opening like hands
we would lay our faces in.
The pink flowering of the mimosa,
the bees hurrying to find the last
of the day's sweetness in each flower.
Butterflies carried on the evening breeze
like the first leaves falling.

After dinner we walk to the pier.
The grown-ups—Grandmother and Aggie,
any relatives who might be visiting
would take our hands and we would lead them
on the familiar path to the water's edge,
sitting on the pier where your mother and
my father played as children, their initials
still carved into the weathered planks.

Overhead, the branches of the old oaks
reach across the sky, interwoven
into a loose fabric of leaves which
wraps us in shadows. The first call
of the owl, the first crickets,
the first few frogs singing
their rusty notes: an old song
played over and over, generation
after generation.

We watch the sun set across the bay
like the lantern of our forefathers
leaving its afterlight of another day.
A pelican swoops low over the horizon,
the place where the sky and the water meet,
that thin distinction now fading.

In the darkness, a silver-backed mullet leaps
from the waves like the arc of the moon
rising. And the moon
beyond the tallest tree appears
like the porch light of heaven
guiding us home.

• • •

All night the mockingbird sings
outside our window, its clear song
sweet and ever-changing. We lie awake
in our beds knowing it is singing for us
though we don't know why or what
it might be saying. But we listen.

From the darkness someone comes to us,
lifting us up, carrying us to the screen porch
where the grown-ups are talking in a small circle
of light. They hold us, rock us,

our faces pressed against the once-starched
summer dresses now soft and wilted against their skin.
Back in our beds, a breeze blows in off the bay,
the air heavily weighted with the scent of jasmine,
gardenia, honeysuckle: the old vines dripping again
with flowers. Someone leans over us, covers us.
We are the dreams of our ancestors waking
and our sleep is ancient and deep.

• • •

They're all here: Grandmother and Aggie
and even my father now.
But my cousin, my youngest cousin,
how could we have known as children
that your grave would be so quickly among them,
that you would take your place among the stones
that bear all of our names. Still,
it can't be terrible to be dead
among those who have loved you for centuries.

The earth here is soft:
it opened for you like the arms of a grandmother
aching with lullabies. The land holds you now,
the land where the azalea and magnolia and camellia
will bloom again and again for others
who will come to call it home.

Laura Gilpin, a regis-
tered nurse, won the
Walt Whitman Award
for *The Hocus-Pocus
of the Universe* and a
fellowship from the
National Endowment
for the Arts. She recently
moved to Alabama,
where her family has
lived since 1810.

There but for the Grace of God

When I'm asked about the meaning of home, two words come to mind: security and love. My generation learned very early in life to cherish both. We were raised during the Depression, and toward the end of the day we often heard a timid knock on the back door and opened it to find a shabby yet scrupulously polite man, cap in hand, asking for food in exchange for odd jobs. We called them hobos, and when I referred to one of them as a bum, my mother reprimanded me sharply. She explained that they were honest, hard-working men down on their luck. They loved their families so much they had chosen to ride the rails looking for work rather than stay at home competing for food along with their wives and children. As poor as we were I cannot remember my mother refusing them. I'm sure she always thought, "There but for the grace of God goes someone I love."

Irene Fencil is a retired nurse and has lived her whole life in Monroe, Wisconsin, with the exception of active duty as a member of the Army Nurse Corps during World War II.

Where Things Can Change

 From childhood I have known that my single greatest accomplishment would be to countermand the abusive effects of six generations of alcoholism. As an adult, I have been even more acutely aware that my home is where an old generation can end, and a new one may begin. Home is where I can teach my son how to have a relationship that honors our individual needs and feelings within a covenant of nonabusive love.

Father

Home is a warm place where you can be loved. Home is where you can sometimes learn things. Home is where you can rest. Home is sometimes a place where things can change.

Son, age ten

Every Summer

 Even though my parents still live in our house, and though there are thirty-four years of memories there, my image of "home" takes me back to a five-minute period that happened every summer, at exactly the same time.

It's late in the afternoon, and L.A. is perfect and cool after a long day of heat. My brother and sister and I have been dropped off in front of our house, home again after our two-week stay up at camp. With duffel bags in tow, we walk in the front door and are immediately confronted with the sweetest, cleanest, most peaceful smell I will ever know. This is the smell of our house when no children are in it. This is our house after my mother has Lemon-Pledged, Mr. Cleaned, swept, and mopped every corner.

This is our house with a calm mother and father, who are happy to see us and who are ready to hear our stories of midnight camp-fires and country dancing. This is our house absent from the chaos of four children, because four children are too many children, even if you do have a maid and can make a mean martini. This is our home after it's taken a break from screaming and scratching and chasing. This is my home, though the memory is brief, and somewhat faded.

Laurie Wagner lives with her husband in a converted metal factory in Oakland, California. She is currently working on a book called *Kindred Spirits*.

---

*Keep the Home
Fires Burning*

*Keep the home fires
    burning,
While your hearts
    are yearning;
Though your lads
    are far away
They dream of home.
There's a silver lining
Through the dark
    cloud shining;
Turn the dark cloud
    inside out
Till the boys come
    home.*

**Lena Guilbert Ford,
1915**

Pieces of a Family

 I have pinned on the wall next to me a lined piece of notebook paper on which is printed, "*I Love You Mom*." It is written in black crayon in the careful hand of a child who might be seven or eight years old.

On the back, in the same black crayon she has drawn a picture of a house with roughly outlined doors and windows. It is almost bleak in its isolation, alone, without life, without warmth, without surroundings.

This piece of paper is special to me. I found it one day along the freeway, in a lot once occupied by a group of homeless people, lying amid the debris of what had been their encampment. Only pieces of their existence remained: a blackened barbecue grill, a paper cup, a few cans, a ragged shirt…and that note.

A woman who works at *Modern Maturity* magazine told me about them. She wasn't sure how long they had been there and didn't know if they were actually a family or simply people thrown together by necessity.

I'm not sure what compelled me to look. Los Angeles' Shelter Partnership estimates that there are up to 80,000 homeless people in the county. Like everyone else, I've gotten used to seeing them around. As long as they aren't intruding on your life, you tend to

East or West, home is best.

Proverb

ignore them. They're like passing traffic, or leaves carried on a
stray wind.

When I got to the place where the freeway family had been, no
one was there. I searched both sides of the freeway and then concen-
trated on an open area near where the encampment had existed.
The day was hot and smoggy, and I wasn't about to spend a lot of
time chasing shadows. But then, as I was walking back toward the
car, a homeless man emerged from a group of eucalyptus trees.

I swear I'd searched the area and hadn't seen anyone, but there
he was, a guy in his late forties, dirty, bearded, and wearing
clothes as old as rainfall. He was vague about almost everything,
but he did point out the exact spot where the family had been.
He'd been there a couple of nights too, until they'd all been told
to move on, though he didn't know by whom. They were always
being told to move. Who told them wasn't important.

The last I saw him, he was walking south along the freeway,
going nowhere.

The hand printed note was in plain sight near the barbecue grill.
I'm pretty sure of the age of the person who wrote it and drew the
picture of a house on the back. I have grandchildren who are seven
and eight, and it looks like something one of them might have done.

I stood there for a long time just looking at the note, drawn
slowly into it, increasingly unaware of the heat and smog. The din
of freeway traffic muted to the distant hum of flies at a picnic

table. I could picture a little girl sitting in the terrible loneliness of the vacant lot, carefully printing the words, and just as meticulously drawing the picture of a home that may have existed in a corner of her memory.

Was there actually a mother for her to write to, or was she just a phantom figure of a child's longing? Had there once been a home, or had all of her young life been spent wandering and dreaming?

The house she drew was a house without her in it, a place beyond the horizons of her reach, cold and distant and empty. It was like one of the real homes that surrounded the vacant lot, viewed through something close to despair.

It takes a heap o' livin' in a house t' make it a home.

Edgar Guest

This is not a good time for the homeless. A growing hostility toward their existence is forcing them out of sight. I think we see their homelessness in ourselves, imagine the utterly devastating failure of spirit they must feel, and simply can't bear the introspection.

I live now with the vision of the child who wrote the note. I always will. One of them may be a little girl whose warmth and loneliness claw at the heart. If so, I hope that she is loved as she loves, because sometimes in the emptiness of a world filled with sadness, love is all we have left.

Al Martinez is a columnist for the Los Angeles Times. His job is to walk among and write about the people—those with faces, and those without.

How to Feel at Home Away from Home

- Pack your friendliest bathrobe and most disreputable slippers.

- Take along small framed photographs of your loved ones and pets for your bedside.

- Take your own alarm clock.

- Make your own brand of coffee or tea in the morning with a special travel kit.

- Indulge in packets of your favorite bath salts for relaxing after your journey.

- Call the people you love on your first night away, or every night if you need to do so.

- Take your own familiar coffee mug or water glass.

- Get your family to fax you a goodnight letter and fax one back to them.

- Unpack special away-from-home guardians to make you feel safe, such as stuffed bears, small rocks from your favorite beach, or little carved figures of animals.

- Buy fragrant flowers for your hotel room.

- Buy fresh fruit to nibble on at night and in the morning.

- Set out your own favorite brand of potpourri in a small elegant bowl.

- Tuck your favorite late night snacks from popcorn to cookies into your suitcase. If you are staying for more than two nights, completely unpack your suitcase and put it away in the closet.

- Fill up the standard hotel-room coffee table with books and magazines or a box of chocolates.

- Buy little presents to take home for your family and make a display of the pretty, wrapped packages.

- Buy postcards and write silly messages on them every night to send home.

- Audiotape your favorite music or a conversation with someone you love.

- Ask your lover or children to record a special audio message for you for when you are alone in your room. Listen to it just before you go to sleep.

- Take along a picture of your home.

- If you are traveling for an extended period, take along a home shrine—a favorite cloth and several small objects that remind you of home.

- If you are staying at a hotel, get to know the employees—the night clerk, doorman, etc. by name. Ask if you can store midnight snacks and beverages in the kitchen.

HOME AS SPIRIT

Turn up the lights.
I don't want to go home in the dark.

O. Henry's last words

Home is a Memory

"When I'm happy my house is a happy place. I eat and have
fun in my house. My house is a place where good things happen
and where bad things happen. My house is a place where I go
when I feel good and mad and sad. When I moved I had mixed
feelings. I was sad to have to leave my old house, but I was happy
I was going to move to a bigger, better house. Now I'm glad I
moved. I feel more safe. I feel happier."

Ariel Boxerman, age nine

"At home I feel lots of mischief and loving kindness. What I love
most about home is just being there."

Garrett Prince, age six

"When I get home from a long day or hard day I like to run
through my home and make sure things are the same as when
I left. The power of home is beyond imagining."

Mathew Merner, age nine

"Home is not just a place where you live. It is memory. Home is a place where you keep how tall you get every year, or just a crack or scratch on the wall. Home is also your family and friends. Even your pet makes you feel that you are at a place where you will never be forgotten."

Maria Ghisletta, age twelve

"Home is a place where I know I want my memories to be. Home is made with love and comfort. I think all the things in my house or anybody's house comes from the heart."

Alida Whitney Peterson, age seven

"A home is not just a place you live in—it's a place you grow up in. I had my best year living in Oita, Japan, in a cold cement apartment. Even if your home is a cold, grey, ugly apartment, it's still a place for memories. The apartment always smelled like fish and garlic. When we came back from a trip, the smell reminded me that we were home."

Christina Flinders, age nine

Coming and Going

For the first thirty years of my life I kept trying to create a "home" with furniture, cookware, tchotchkes, and intimate friends. Those years had great moments of hominess, but there were a lot of other moments as well.

In 1961, I was catapulted into another dimension of consciousness through ingesting Teonanactyl (flesh of the Gods), the sacramental mushroom of Mexico. Within my mind, layer by layer, I shed my social and psychological identities until a moment of panic when I seemed to cease to exist. The next moment I was infused with a deep joy and peace that was of a profundity that I had never known in this lifetime.

When I was finally able to speak, the first words I uttered were, "I'm home."

Years later I was on a long tour and arrived at yet another Holiday Inn. As I sat down in the impersonal room, I thought, "Only two more weeks and I can go home."

When I heard myself think that, I saw inherent in that statement a cause of suffering. So I got up, took the key, went out and closed the door, and walked down the hall. Then I retraced my steps to the motel room door, opened it, and yelled, "I'm home!"

Be thou thine own home, and in thy self dwell.

John Donne

112

Since then I don't experience ever leaving home. As Hakuin, the Zen poet, said, "Your coming and going is nowhere but where you are."

Ram Dass is an internationally known author and lecturer. He has written ten books, including *Be Here Now* and *Compassion in Action*. In 1978 he co-founded the Seva Foundation, an international service organization working in public health and social justice issues in communities throughout the world.

The Equation for Love

 I was in Thalheim, a small German farm town north of Frankfurt, to receive darshan from Mother Meera. Mother Meera is a Hindu avatar, a person who is believed to be the incarnation of the divine. She doesn't speak to the thousands of pilgrims from around the world who come to receive her blessing, but instead, as you kneel before her, she holds the back of your head for about thirty seconds. My friend James tells me that she is untying the karmic knots she sees in the lines that run up the back of your body. Then she looks you in the eyes, bobbing her head slightly, for maybe a minute. She is in her thirties and very beautiful, with large brown eyes and a bold red tika painted in the middle of her forehead. You go kind of giddy looking at her, and your bones relax. James tells me she is pulling white light down from the center of the universe and pouring it into your body. Who knows? It feels good. And I've never been one to turn down white light from the center of the universe.

It was my last day in Thalheim and I had hours on my hands before the evening darshan so I packed my water colors and an apple into my backpack and headed for the lake. A paved bicycle path cut through cultivated fields and patches of symmetrically planted dark forest. Berry bushes lined the trail, offering their goods if you dared reach into the thorny vines that tattoo your arms with their signature.

At the top of the hill, a cherry tree ripe with red fruit held court in the middle of a green field. There were no fences. I stood under the tree and picked cherries, paying attention to the color and shape of each piece, looking to identify the characteristics of sweetness. I studied the cherries in my hand. They were luminous with plump color, almost singing. In that moment, something happened. I saw that food is made out of light. If you take a moment to look, it's obvious, scientific, the way a physicist has a vision and then spends his life finding the equation for it. I bit into a cherry to test my theory. The sweet of it burst inside of me, like red love. In that moment, I understood that the cherry needed me to be fulfilled in its life, to appreciate the taste of cherry. The cherry needed my tongue, my lips, to complete its destiny in this world. Not just to spit out the pits so cherries can go on forever like they teach you in high school biology class. Cherries need our eyes to know their beauty, our mouths to delight in their juicy flavor, our bellies to sigh with appreciation. In that moment I knew that with tongue, touch, smell, ears, teeth, bones, sinew, I belonged to this earth. The sweet taste of cherry was the proof.

Ever wonder why it's bad luck to open an umbrella inside a house? The pagodas built as religious temples for Buddha in India were architecturally derived from the image of pyramiding parasols. To open an umbrella inside became a symbol of disrespect to Buddha, and therefore bad luck.

Nina Wise is a performance artist and writer from Marin County, California. She is a practicing Jewish Buddhist with a Hindu guru and has spent much of her life wondering what to call home.

Looking Out My Kitchen Window
in Late June

In my garden, new flies spiral in the sun
like small white parachutes against the thick
dark vines. The orange trumpet flowers spill over
and over the wall. The house is still.
The kitchen smells of peaches. Outside: summer,
swelling like a wave. For a moment,
there is nothing that I want.

Carolyn Miller and
her cat Louie Louie live
in a Dashiell Hammett-
kind of flat in a Romeo-
and-Juliet-style building
in San Francisco. She is
a poet, book editor, and
writer and publishes a
small magazine named
VIVO.

Weaving Our History

Once, many years ago, when I was a child, I visited an old, widowed neighbor every afternoon after school. I called her Auntie Bea, and as soon as I had laid my books down on the kitchen table and changed from my school clothes, I climbed over the rough masonry wall separating our gardens and called to her as I ran to her kitchen door. She always welcomed me in, often with a glass of milk and cookies, sometimes with delicious soft dried apricots or fruit candies she kept in a large glass jar next to her chair. Once, when I came, she was opening a package, and as she pushed aside the tissue paper, she gave an exclamation of joy. "Oh," she said, "oh how lovely." I don't remember the color or the size of the silk scarf that she held up; all I remember is her removing her wedding ring and, like a magician, passing the scarf through it, and so finely woven and so delicately fashioned was that scarf that it seemed to float through the round, gold cylinder of her ring.

Later, when I was older, I met a young Japanese man who had come to America. He left his grandparents and parents in tears and dismay, for he had flaunted all custom by deserting his birthright as the eldest son. He often described his ancestral home, with its bamboo framing, its tatami mats, its sliding doors

What is the use of a house if you don't have a decent planet to put it on?

Henry David Thoreau

117

paned with delicate rice paper. What he remembered most from his childhood was his duty of feeding mulberry leaves to the silkworms housed in the warmth of the dark, shadowy attic, and how as a very small child he was frightened by the noise of all the worms chewing on the leaves. He described the sound of their mouths chewing, chewing, chewing, their hunger insatiable until they had wound themselves up into their silken homes. After they emerged, he and his brothers and sisters gathered up the silk cases for their grandmother, who dyed them and unwound the silken threads in rainbow strands of color.

Now as an adult, these two stories weave together in me, the rough scrape of the masonry on my knee as I scrambled over the wall, the silky scarf, the hungry worms, and my own life the intersection of such disparate experiences. As we live our lives, we fill with memories and we create the histories that we display in the rooms where we live. Our homes are woven from our past lives and future hopes. The warp and weft is spun from gently handling our grandmother's silver, serving tradition on our aunt's best pie plate, living out the past sitting on our grandfather's leather stool, growing into the future gently dusting our own treasured childhood toys. Closets filled with clothes mark the seasons with coats for nippy nights, bathing suits for summer weekends at the beach,

One face to the world, another at home makes for misery.
Amy Vanderbilt,
New Complete Book
of Etiquette

sweats for lounging around with coffee and the morning newspaper on Sundays. Like the long flights of migrating birds, the dance of the honeybee, the life cycle of the silkworm, we lay down patterns along lines of memories. Our homes become the center of the dervish whirl of our life, and its intersecting lines cross at our doorstep. From remembered kindnesses of love, to the passive ticking of time, to the tinkering thoughts of hopes and dreams, all are spun together with the effort of love, the pain of memory, and the pleasure of expectation.

Mary Gumpertz lives in New Orleans, Louisiana with an African gray parrot named Jerry who dances on his perch when you sing to him.

Fire-Proof

 In October 1991, the most destructive residential fire in U.S. history ripped across the Oakland, California hills. Twenty-four people were killed, and 2,991 dwellings burnt to the ground within twelve hours. Eight of the twenty-four people, including my neighbor, died on the narrow and beautiful road where I once lived. My home was one of the first structures to be consumed by the 4,000 degree flames that jumped from house to house in five seconds flat. By the end of the day, thousands of people were homeless.

I am an intensely private person, and so when the boundaries between public and private spaces shattered that day I instantly became lost in a series of relentless panic attacks. The day-to-day experience of dealing with all the bureaucracies, phone calls, and paperwork was maddening. Add to this a general sense of disorientation and displacement and the result felt like a kind of hell. Simple tasks such as replacing my toothbrush and contact lens case felt overwhelming. My sleep cycle was totally disrupted, and the cliché "running on empty" took on new meaning.

In spite of all this, I can confidently say that the fire changed and enriched my life. The experience of being burned out has helped bring my life into a new focus. I look very differently at the concepts of property and ownership, and I know that many good things emerge out of sad and painful events. All the objects that were once so important to me are not nearly as important as the lessons I learned. Out of destruction has come great beauty along with touching gestures of generosity and kindness. The mind's tendency to label experience as one thing or another has never seemed so limited as it appears to me now. During my more mindful moments, I see the fire as no more bad than good, no more a tragedy than a gift.

Technically, the fire left me homeless. There was no structure for me to return to or possessions to call my own. It's easy to believe that things like walls, books, beds, and closets make up a home. But when it is all reduced down to a thick pile of ashes, you are compelled to reconsider where your real home is. The truth is, I was never homeless. As long as I am in this moment, I am no more a person without a home than I am a person without a past. Every moment is our true home. The moment is fire-proof. It needs no down payment, insurance policy, or alarm system. All we need to do is live there.

Ronna Kabatznick, social psychologist, founded and directs Dieters Feed the Hungry, a nonprofit organization based in Berkeley, California. She is a vipassana meditator, and lives with her husband in a house with a wonderful rose garden. She is the author of the forthcoming book *The Zen of Eating*.

Every radish I ever pulled up seemed to have a mortgage attached to it.

Ed Wynn, explaining why he sold his farm

Redefining Home

 When I got married at age twenty-one, I adopted my husband's definition of home: "Home is when we are together whether we stay or whether we go."

When my husband went to serve in Vietnam, there was no more home because we were not together. When he died there, the possibility of ever having a home with him disappeared. I had to create a new home. And that I did with my baby girl, who was born two months after his death. She and I had a home for twenty-five years. Last year, I walked her down the aisle to meet her new life partner and she created a home for herself. I had to redefine home again.

I finally found my real home. It matters not where I am sleeping, eating, or keeping my toothbrush. I come home to myself every day by taking time to reunite with my inner essence. When I honor my feelings, respect myself, listen to the whisperings of my heart, I am home. Being home is being at peace with myself, my world, and my life.

Pauline Laurent is a consultant, public speaker, and writer who is currently working on a book about self-care, creativity, and unresolved grief. She says she was forty-seven years old the first time she ever lived alone. It took her a long time to find and have a home of her own.

Everybody's always talking about people breaking into houses… but there are more people in the world who want to break out of houses.

Thorton Wilder

A State of Mind and Heart

 Home is more feeling than concept—not so much a place as a state of mind and heart. Home is a soft voice, a loving touch, a sense of sanctuary, where I can be myself, naked, in all my humanity, all my faults, foibles, and capacity.

My ability to feel "at home" mirrors my ability to commune with the present moment. I've felt "home" in an act of sexual love, in the forest, in an old apartment house when the sun's rays angled through a dusty pane and God touched my face. In moments of repose, when the mind stills, I feel at home in my body, in the mystery of life.

Dan Millman, a former world-champion gymnast, coach, and college professor, has written many books, including *The Way of the Peaceful Warrior, Sacred Journey, No Ordinary Moments, The Life You Were Born to Live,* as well as two books for children.

Seers started off gazing into still lakes and streams to see the future, but switched their technology when mirrors became available. Simpler people believed that the picture they saw in the mirror was a reflection of their soul. If a mirror broke, the soul was lost, and death was soon to follow. That is why we still feel uneasy seeing a mirror broken in shards.

The Center

My center moves with me. Having been raised on the edge of the great North American prairie, my center is a horizon-to-horizon infinity of sun-browned, late summer grass. The keen-edged blades hiss and brush against each other as wind-driven troughs and crests pass; the air is alive with the susurration of insects.

The exact physical place could never be found outside of my mind's image, though a short after-work drive or pedal could carry any inhabitant of a town or city to a place alike to it in spirit if not in kind. My own life's circumstances, like anyone's, have carried me far, to ocean coasts and Arctic villages. And with every step taken or mile driven, in quiet moments, when my eyes stray to places I've passed in looks back or glances to the rearview mirror, I see that place in my mind's eye as I search for the reassurance of constancy and security.

To some, to stand upon the prairie, the heartland, is to stand apart from it. Yet home means acceptance, and for that surroundings must be embraced and incorporated into the flesh. To stand upon the prairie is to be exposed, naked, vulnerable. There's fear and trembling in that. Homesteaders have been driven mad by the plain raw emptiness. They failed to make the place their home,

Anywhere I hang my heart is home…it's just the closet that keeps moving.

Wavy Gravy

124

their image of a center. Part of accepting such an elemental land-scape into one's heart is a letting go of the barriers between the self and the land, a release and exposure of the heart. The heart expands, wind-driven, to absorb the horizons and in turn be absorbed by the thirsty soil. As Wallace Stegner observed, it is both humbling and awe-inspiring to carry a piece of such infinity.

Roots can be tested, grasses tugged. The soil can be crumbled and allowed to sift through fingers. The wind can be breathed for hints of smoke or rain. Stones, whether water-polished cobbles or cracked shale, can be overturned like thoughts, rubbed, weighed by careful heft, kept, or tossed down. Here, at the center within, the storms roll overhead, lash rain and pelt hail, but pass in gusts and the diminishing mutter of thunder. The center remains: sanctuary, source, home.

Ian Cameron Esslemont lived for five winters in Fairbanks, Alaska, in cabins without plumbing or running water. Armed with a flashlight and toilet paper he made frantic dashes to outhouses all ten winter months long. He is looking for-ward to a new job in rural Thailand and hopes to continue the tradition, only now dashing through tropical downpours.

So it's home again,
*   and home again,*
America for me
My heart is turning
*   home again*
And there I long to be.
Henry Van Dyke

A Moment of Safety

 In the evening, I sink down into the ocean of hot water and sea salts. The scented candle dances in the corner and watches. Sedated, I snuggle under the clean, cool sheets, and the weight of the quilt my mother stitched atop the heavy pink comforter swaddling me like a newborn; I am at home as I sigh with deep relief and disappear into my subconscious world. Dwelling in a moment of safety, at peace, feeling free and light, I am at home.

Mary Ellen Rescigno works for a firm that assists the development of low-income housing throughout California.

A Little While More

As a Buddhist monk, I am a home leaver. The ordination ceremony for Buddhist monks is called the "leaving home" ceremony. In it the practitioner formally leaves his or her home and family and takes on a wandering homeless life of freedom in which one is to give one's love not to one group only but to all beings, and one is to rest not in a particular place but in consciousness itself.

But even before that, as a Jew, I was raised with a constant sense of dislocation. We were well aware that our people had come from elsewhere (not from a home country, just another country) than northeastern Pennsylvania and that at a moment's notice we would go elsewhere if it were necessary to do so. Each year at Passover time the deep image of our wandering nature was reviewed in the Exodus story of packing up in the middle of the night and hurriedly going. As soon as I was old enough I left home. I have never returned and I do not expect that I'll ever go back.

Yet I carry a persistent image of home with me wherever I go. When I travel to teach meditation retreats, I feel it most: my meditation cushion and my few belongings, neatly laid out and cared for, these are home for me. My robes, and my own body and mind responding to this bright world—these are home.

Oddly enough, I live, with my wife and twin sons, in one of the most beautiful places on earth, the hills of Marin County, near the Pacific Ocean. When I came I planned on staying for just a while, and it still feels like I just arrived and will be staying just a little while more, though it has been fifteen years. Somehow it has become my home.

Norman Fischer is a Zen Buddhist priest who once lived in a monastery. Today he lives in a Zen Buddhist community in Sausalito, California. He is the author of several volumes of poetry, his latest being *Precisely the Point Being Made.*

Home at Last

 In times of pain and disappointment, my response has been to move. My last big journey was from Boston to San Francisco thirteen years ago. It took me until this year to drive roots through the hard-packed soil of old memories and feelings, a legacy of my upbringing. I've let go of a lot: my ties with family members, my painful memories. I bought a modest house, had a child, and peopled my life with loving, unique friends. All these things have nurtured roots it would take a nuclear blast to displace. When the old behavior pattern crosses my conscious mind, I think, "Move? Move where? I am home." Amen.

ND Wilson helps people obtain financing to purchase their homes. She particularly enjoys working with first-time buyers who are traumatized yet excited by the whole transaction and particularly grateful when they get their financing.

"My God and my mother live in the West, and I will not leave them. It is a tradition of my people that we never cross the three rivers—the Grande, the San Juan, the Colorado. Nor could I leave the Chuska Mountains, I was born there. I shall remain. I have nothing to leave but my life, but I will not move."
Manuelito of the Navahos in a speech given to Congress, 1865

Around the World and Around Again

 As a traveler by nature, I am motivated by a boundless curiosity about the world. The ship's horn, the train's whistle, sounds that to others may sound mournful—these, to me, are shouts of joy. My greatest pleasure is in being not at home; not comfortable, not habituated, not sleepwalking though a life made dull by repetition. For me, then, homecoming and departure are reversed. It's coming "home" that brings a sense of loss, of melancholy.

The process of moving about the world has worked a change. As I begin to return repeatedly to certain places in my travels, I discover an unexpected sense of homecoming, a quickening of the heartbeat having no connection, necessarily, with expected pleasure. Home has become Singapore, New Delhi, Athens, Papeete, Pago-Pago, Kathmandu. Edinburgh, Mont St. Michel, the Engadine. Bali, Hydra, Fiji. And on and on, around the world and around again.

And this is what the traveler discovers: in this great and endlessly fascinating world of ours, everywhere can be home.

Meredith Moraine has fulfilled many of her travel dreams: working on a Norwegian freighter in the South Pacific, herding cows in Switzerland, hitching train rides in the Canadian Rockies, hiking the Himalayas, living in Bali, and much more.

Sanctuary

 When I first entered the gates of San Quentin in the winter of 1981, I walked across the upper yard holding my "fish kit" of prison-issued belongings. I saw the faces of hundreds of prisoners who had already made the prison their home. I watched them all staring at me with their piercing eyes, their rugged faces and beards of all different shades—all dressed in their prison blue jeans and worn coats, some with cigarettes hanging from their lips, others with black glasses covering their eyes, leaning against the chain fences.

I will never forget the moment when the steel cell door slammed loudly shut behind me. I stood in the middle of the darkness trying to fix my eyes and readjust the thoughts that were telling me that this was not home and that this tiny space would not, could not be the place where I would spend more than a decade of my life. My mind kept saying, "No! Hell no!" to all this. I thought again of all those hundreds of rugged-faced prisoners I had seen in the yard moments ago, who looked so old and so accustomed to their fates.

Standing there, I dropped my fish kit. I opened my arms and realized that the palms of my hands touched the walls with ease. Before I knew it I was pushing against them with all my might,

When you're safe at home you wish you were having an adventure; when you're having an adventure you wish you were safe at home.

Thornton Wilder

until I realized how silly it was to think that these thick concrete walls were somehow going to budge. I went to find the light switch. It was placed on the back wall, only a few feet above the steel-plated bunk. The bed was bolted into the wall like a flat shelf. It was only two and one-half feet by six feet long, and the bed was several feet above the gray concrete floor.

My eyes had adjusted to the darkness by the time that I turned on the lights. But what I hadn't seen until then was the hundreds upon hundreds of cockroaches that were clustered all about, especially around the combined toilet and sink appliance on the back wall. All the roaches suddenly scattered. They dashed into all the tiny holes and cracks behind the sink and in the walls. They all disappeared, leaving only the very fat and young roaches still running scared. I was beyond shock to see so many of these nasty creatures. And although it was not true, I began feeling roaches climbing all over me. I even imagined them mounting a counter attack against me when I was asleep.

This was home. For hours I couldn't bear the thought. The hundreds of roaches, all the top-to-bottom filth covering the walls, the balls of dirt clustered on the floor, and the awful smell of urine that had been left in the toilet for God knows how long all sickened me to the point of nearly passing out.

To find home in San Quentin I had to first find an unbelievable
will to survive. My first domestic action in this direction was to
flush the toilet. Surprisingly, all the necessities to clean the cell
were in the fish kit. In it, I found a towel, a face cloth, one bar of
state soap, a tooth brush, and a comb; a small can of powdered
toothpaste, a box of state detergent, and a small plastic cup. There
were also two National Geographic magazines that were twenty
years old, one of them from the exact month and year of my birth.

It seemed that time was now on my side. I took to cleaning
vigorously. I started with only one wall, scrubbing it from top to
bottom, and then moved on to the next, scrubbing as hard as I
could to remove all the markings and filth plastered over them.
I scrubbed each of the walls down to the floor. I didn't stop.
I figured that if I had to sleep here, this was the least I could do.
I went on scrubbing until the walls were spotless. The cell bars,
sink, toilet, and floor all got the same treatment.

For hours, sometimes on my hands and knees, I washed down
and scrubbed every inch of my cell—including the ceiling, once
I found the creative means to climb to the highest wall to get at
the filth. When the whole cell was spotless, I was convinced that
I could eat a dropped piece of candy from my floor. There was
not a single spot or marking on either wall. The roaches had all

Returning Home

I have arrived.
I am home.
In the here.
In the now.
I am solid.
I am free.
In the ultimate, I dwell.
                    Thich Nhat Hanh

133

drowned in the floor or been killed. I solved the problem of their hiding places by plugging up the holes and cracks behind the walls with toilet paper. I wet the paper into balls, and then stuffed them tightly into all the cracks. The toilet was another real concern to me. I had heard about prisoners being compelled to wash their faces in these very toilets when tear gas is shot into the units to break up mass disruptions and the water is purposely shut off by the authorities. I imagined my face going inside this toilet, and I cleaned it to the highest military standards.

After the first days had passed, I decided to decorate my walls with photographs taken out of the National Geographic magazines. The landscape of Malaysia and other parts of the world had enormous beauty to them. And I gladly plastered them about everywhere. These small tokens of life on the walls helped me to imagine a life beyond the walls of a prison.

After a while, I realized that home seemed to be what I could make of it. Over the years, I collected books and even got a television and radio to be my windows to the outside world. And I have pasted many thousands of photographs on the walls throughout these past thirteen years. The one that has made my home in prison the most like a sanctuary is a very small photograph of the "Bodhisatt" Buddha that a very dear friend on the outside sent in to me. It has been in the center of my wall for a number of years now. And I always begin my prison day through the practice of meditation, sitting on the cold floor each morning, cushioned only by my neatly folded blanket. There, I always welcome the light of morning and realize, as though I were seeing through clouds, that home is genuinely wherever the heart can be found.

Jarvis Masters is an African American writer who lives on death row in San Quentin State Prison. He is a frequent contributor to *Turning Wheel*, and has been published in *Men's Studies Review*, *Recovering*, *Men's Counsel Newsletter*, *Wingspan*, and other publications. He received a 1992 PEN Center writing award in poetry.

Homesick

 My first home shattered under the weight of
parental alcoholism when I was six. Oklahoma
made me a ward of the state and sent me to its
only Catholic orphanage, St. Patrick's Indian Mission in dusty
Anadarko. The next three years are dark in memory; I wet my bed
a lot. Eventually I snapped out of it; reading Huck Finn helped.

In the orphanage, we were a stoic lot; boxing was our only sport.
But we recognized one—and only one—emotion that required
that someone be given a break: homesickness. "Don't bother
him, he's homesick."

When I was forty-four, attempting once more to jump-start my
sputtering theatrical career, I asked myself, why am I running?
Why have I been struggling all these years to become rich and
famous? What do I really want? Finally the light went on: the kid
from the orphanage wants a home! Riches and fame would bring
the right woman, who would of course make me a home.

I was tired of waiting, so I decided to make a home for myself.
I bought my first cookbook, dishes, matching towels, a bed, a
bookcase. Now, fourteen years later, my bread-and-butter pickles
are famous, cut flowers from my garden grace my desk and mantel-

piece, and my fig-ginger jam is legendary. Making myself at home —in my own skin, in my house, or in the universe—turned out to be an inside job. I needed to do it for myself rather than wait for someone to do it for me.

Our weary, alienated nation suffers from nearly universal homesickness; we are a nation of orphans. Many believe that we cannot have a home without a partner or a mortgage. Against this some of us have chosen to affirm that right where we are is enough. Homemaking remains the true, perennial center of the only civilized life that really matters. Now, I call myself a homemaker.

John Argue was born in Tulsa, Oklahoma. He is a professional actor and a teacher of movement for people with Parkinson's disease. He makes his home in Albany, California.

It was the best place to be, thought Wilbur, this warm delicious cellar with the garrulous geese, the changing seasons, the heat of the sun, the passage of swallows, the nearness of rats, the sameness of sheep, the love of spiders, the smell of manure, and the glory of everything.

E.B. White,
Charlotte's Web

A Place to Become Yourself

 Home is a place where you can catch a dream and ride it to the end of the line and back. Where you can watch shadow and light doing a tight little tango on a wooden floor or an intoxicated moon rising through an empty window. Home is a place to become yourself. It's the right spot, the bright spot, or just the spot where you can land on your feet or recline in a tub of sparkling brew if you're so inclined. It's a place of silence where harmony and chaos are shuffled like a deck of cards and it's your draw. It's somewhere you can close a door and open your heart.

Theo Pelletier was born in Brooklyn, New York. Although he now lives 3,000 miles away, the east coast is still a large part of his life. He has written several short stories, including one that he co-wrote which became the story for the motion picture *Mr. Baseball*.

To Go Home

 The clearest understanding of home came to me when my husband Fred had a serious car accident that left him with a double fracture of his left leg, a punctured lung, and concussion. The police told me that when they arrived, Fred was walking—on a broken leg—and told them, "My name is Fred Cody and I want to go home."

He was delirious for three days and, despite his injuries, repeatedly tried to get out of his bed in the intensive-care unit "to go home." He did not mention me or our four children by name: we were implicit in "home." We had built a world together (in that house), a world that was part of the fabric of our individual being.

My children are adults now and each one has their own home, but they continue to speak of "home for the holidays" when we are all together in our first home.

Pat Cody was co-owner of Cody's Bookstore, the famed heart of intellectual life in Berkeley, California. A health educator, she and her husband encouraged, stimulated, and supported scores of writers, all while making a home for their own family.

Home

Home is a place
in a land
in a town
in a house
in a room
in me.
Home is the place
I come home to.
Home is a place
where I can just sit
and think.
Home is a place
inside by the fire
where I watch the flames
or read a book
or outside by a tree
in a sweet little place
that I love to be.
Home is a place
in a land in a town
in a house in a room
in me.

Sarah Hodges is ten
years old. She lives
in Tomales, California
with her mom, dad,
two sisters, two brothers,
a Siamese bunny, two
cats, some chickens and
a goldfish. She goes to a
one-room school, where
her mom is the teacher.

A Way Home

 You Want Have Sleep This House Please Don't Take Anytink… This crudely lettered message nailed to the door of a trapper's log cabin near the headwaters of the Yukon River was a harbinger of lessons in bush hospitality whose frequent repetition would enrich my idea of what a home can be. The summer I kayaked down the river I stopped in every village and visited dozens of homesteads and fish camps. Along the way I began to learn what it means to be a stranger and a guest. There were times when people actually vied with one another to offer me a meal or a place to stay. I once arrived in a village after midnight and was treated to a full-course meal and a display of family photographs. When the salmon runs began, I seldom departed without an ample supply of fresh or smoked fish for the journey. Salmon became the very currency of hospitality.

One story goes that the salmon live in three great lodges in the sea, one for each of the three Yukon species that follows the ancient imperative to return to the freshwater streams of their birth: Chinook, Coho, and Chum. It is said that they are traveling to a potlatch, a gift exchange, and are willingly lured into the people's weirs and nets thinking that they are gifts. If well treated by their "hosts" and prepared and shared with respect, their spirits

We have to stumble through so much dirt and humbug before we reach home. And we have no one to guide us. Our only guide is our homesickness.

Hermann Hesse,
Steppenwolf

141

will return to the lodges and tell the story of their reception, and others will follow. The salmon runs will continue and the people will continue as well.

The salmon struggled upriver. I paddled and drifted down, each day taking me farther from home than I had ever been before. I began encountering people who spoke little or no English. My hosts seemed to particularly relish my willingness to try what was for me increasingly exotic food: bear steaks, pickled beaver tail, loon soup. I began to notice something strange. Not only were people treating me like family…they were beginning to look like family! I met Eskimo elders who reminded me of my grandmother and her sisters, Russian Jews who emigrated west to America and retained in their features faint suggestions of Siberian heritage. Other Russians had traveled east, trading their way up the Yukon in the 1830s, sometimes marrying the Yupik and Athabaskan people they encountered. Old women stood for hours by the riverbank cutting salmon into strips and hanging them on wooden racks to dry…I felt warmth and recognition in their smiling eyes, and remembered that my grandmother always cooked smoked salmon and eggs for me when I visited, and that on my many returns to my parents' house lox was always the "welcome home" breakfast.

To market to market
to buy a fat pig
Home again home
again, jiggety-jig.
Nursery Rhyme

With the weather getting colder and wetter as I neared the coast, the hours and the days ceded their names to the flow of the river. It was the end of a three-month journey and I was on "river time." I prepared breakfast over one of my last campfires and remembered Thoreau's saying that he who cuts his own wood is twice warmed. Biting into a piece of hard-smoked salmon with its rich coppery oil dribbling down my chin, I knew that just a few mouthfuls would warm me and sustain a morning's paddle into the wind. I also knew that this gift and countless acts of hospitality I had received would sustain me for a lifetime. People had not simply opened their homes to me. They had shown me how to make my own home larger, how to open it to others…family, friends, strangers, and finally to myself. They had shown me a way home.

Bob Kanegis is a professional storyteller who encourages people to appreciate their own and other's stories through the creation of "the endangered stories act." He is a self-described geographic schizophrenic who loves every place he has ever lived. Smoked salmon is still his favorite food.

Crossing the threshold meant many things in the old days. To stumble in crossing foretold disaster, so always step carefully when entering a house. For example, legend has it that Tiberius Gracchus stumbled on the threshold of his home and died the same day.

My Own Shore

 Hotel room surfaces. Other people have passed or will pass here, as early as tomorrow morning, as recently as yesterday. Fitting their coat to the hanger, dropping their toothbrush to the counter, unpacking their socks away in the drawer, they will finger the television programmer and flip through the channels, to stop at the local Eye Witness News and, like me, miss the cadences of home. A train will pass like a cliché in the night and a wake-up call will leave them groggy and confused. Each transfer from plane to plane, from baggage claim to the yellow cab, is like a crest I must ride to the shore of my home. That city apartment with my cedar hope chest, the books stacked on the hardwood floor, the tree branches scraping solemnly against my wide windows, the broad-based lamp that still remains from my divorce, the musty smell of the rain where it slides from the crack in the bedroom window to the floorboards each winter, the scattered pieces of myself arranged in comfortable heaps and protruding from drawers. I charge up the stairs. I turn each of the three keys and push the door open, holding my breath. I flick the light and drag my suitcase inside, shut the door, and bolt it, and breathe in this tender air that has been waiting just for me.

Vicki Morgan travels extensively on business and knows first-hand about longing to be home.

A Rooted Heart

 I don't know what it means to be at home because
from the age of seven I became an exile and had to
leave the place, so close to the land, the river, and
the sky, where I was born. For me, not being at home is like bleed-
ing from a very deep wound—so deep that you don't even know
that you are wounded.

It is like looking desperately to find fertile soil to plant your
roots. You know that it has to be found soon, because some of the
roots are drying and withering. You can feel the cool edge of dying.
But there is no soil, no ground, no earth—just pavement.

It is like having a dozen fertile eggs, trying to find a quiet and
safe place for them to nest, and not finding anything but predators.

What else can I do but plant the roots in my own heart? And
that's what I did: I put the eggs in a nest between the arteries and
veins, and let the blood of my wound warm and nourish them.

For me, and for others who come from natural environments
that have been destroyed by civilization, "home" as a physical
place is gone forever. Maybe the roots, the heart, the eggs, and
the blood are symbols of a new paradigm emerging for us.

Noris Binet Cortés recently returned home to the Dominican Republic after
an absence of eighteen years. She is the author of *Women on the Inner Journey*,
and has opened a gallery of women's art in Nashville.

Where They Can't Kick You Out

 When I was a teenager, the saying "Home is where, when you go there, they can't kick you out" acquired a real meaning for me.

I was eleven when my family moved from Brooklyn, New York, to San Diego. Culturally speaking, you couldn't have found two more perfect opposites—not just in terms of big city versus small-ish town, but in terms of the cultural makeup of the neighborhoods and schools I knew. I'd gone from an entirely Italian-American district with thousands of tenement dwellers on each block to a formless expanse of postwar tract houses inhabited largely by a motley collection of families who seemed to have no ethnicity whatsoever. Back in Brooklyn we all knew the same languages, went to the same churches, rooted for the same teams, ate the same food. In San Diego I learned there were some people who not only weren't Catholic, but had no religion at all. It was culture shock, pure and simple, and it took me years to reorient myself.

During those first, difficult years in San Diego the one saving grace in my life was home. Life in my family was no idyll; we were prone to all the shouting and emotionality that comes with being Italian, and there were stresses on my parents resulting from our move, my father starting his career over, and so on. But I always felt that, no matter what had gone on at school, when I returned home I would be accepted for who I was. The people there (and the people who came to visit, now that I think about it) loved me, encouraged me, appreciated me for my talents, and didn't mock me for my shortcomings—unlike the often unforgiving kids at school.

Those bewildering junior high years taught me the value of the outsider's perspective, and something even more important: that there is a place, somewhere in this world, for each of us, that no matter how little agreement or support or approval you receive from the world at large, a dollop of welcome can suffice to make you feel wanted and loved. And beyond that, when times are really tough or when everyone around you seems to think you're loony, it is even possible to provide that welcome, that support, that at-homeness, for yourself. Because if you have even once had the experience of being welcomed, loved, and accepted, you've been told that you are welcome-able, lovable, acceptable; and that can become the basis for what sometimes seems like the most elusive thing in our modern world—self-esteem, and access to the power that comes with it.

In our over-mediafied, hyper-politicized, consumption-driven society, we've not only lost touch with each other, we've lost touch with ourselves, and any sense of where we fit into the Big Picture. I first began to acquire a sense of my place on the cosmic map when I encountered the work of Buckminster Fuller, the famous designer

Ah, what is more blessed than to put cares away, when the mind lays by its burden, and tired with labor of far travel we have come to our own home and rest on the couch we longed for? This it is which alone is worth all these toils.

Catullus, 87–54 B.C.

of the geodesic dome. Although on the face of it his work was based in rational thought and the scientific method, he was at heart a mystic whose every scientific discovery led him to a kind of spiritual rapture at the intricacy and perfection of the world's "design." Hearing him explain molecular architecture, for example, it was sometimes hard to follow him scientifically, but it was easy to be infected with his sense of being "at home in the Universe." You began to share his awe at how well the structures and processes of nature worked. (My favorite Bucky quote: "You never hear Universe say 'I'm not ready.' Universe never says, 'I don't know what to do about that.'") And you began to see that that perfect design was also at work in you.

In the last analysis, the only place you have to feel at home— the only place you can feel at home—is within yourself. Houses can burn up or fall down; material success comes and goes; relationships can wither away; everything in this world changes. The only thing you carry around with you every moment of your life is your sense of who you are. If you are comfortable with who you are, you can find your home—indeed, you are already home. And no one can kick you out.

Phil Catalfo is a contributing editor of New Age Journal and Whole Earth Review. He is presently writing *All God's Children: Raising a Spiritual Child in a Material World*. He feels at home in the universe in Berkeley, California.

Home is the Land

I've hiked up Mrs. Pieromarchi's hill across the road, and from here I sit dreamily in the warm autumn sunshine gazing out over our land, the twenty-acre ranch we purchased so impulsively when we were first married well over a decade ago. It was growing prunes when we bought it. Now it grows wine grapes. The vines cascade in contoured rows down the steep hillsides. Today their leaves are all the warm colors in the spectrum, from yellow to red-purple.

We must cultivate our garden.

Voltaire

My eyes follow the road past the winery, to the top of the hill. Around the bend, flanked by redwoods, tucked under an umbrella of majestic oak trees, is our house. Its basic structure is that of a solid log cabin. It is unpretentious. It has been expanded from time to time to meet the needs of those who lived there. It is in need of repairs at the moment, but is still sound and cozy.

My vegetable garden is surely the heart of the land for me. It has taught me to be still and listen attentively, to be open and receptive to the natural cycles of growth and change. It has given me insights and the awareness that insight is not in and of itself change. It has brought me home to the depths of my heart.

Arlene Bernstein is a practicing psychotherapist and retreat facilitator who was a co-founder and former owner of Mount Veeder Winery in Napa, California. Her book, *A Growing Season*, is scheduled for a Fall 1995 release.

149

There Becomes Home

Anadarko rests on the banks of the Washita, downriver a ways from the place where the Seventh Cavalry descended on Black Kettle's band of Cheyennes. Blood flowed past Caddo and Kiowa and Wichita homes through Oklahoma, red earth, rushing toward the Red River and redemption. The Baptists, still hell-bent on saving savages a hundred years later, commissioned my parents to Wichita Mission in hopes of finishing the job. Anadarko—home of Indian City USA, of the Redskin Theater, of my Aunt Bertha Pickard who endured it all—is not my home just because I was born there. There becomes home when you learn to walk on your own two feet, when you call the dogs and they come, when you survive the killing fever.

• • •

"Where you from?"

"South Dakota," I said, "Rapid City."

"I've been there." He smiled. "Stopped at Mt. Rushmore on the way to Yellowstone. Took lots of pictures. Seemed like it'd be a nice place to grow up."

Yes, I thought to myself, but there's more to it than colonial meditations at the Shrine of Democracy, pilgrim. Your drive-by shootings aimed low and missed the backyard barbecues, the tree fort, the sledding in winter, the funerals for favored gerbils, and the spectacular view from the top of the hill, looking down on the Interstate and your tiny car speeding by too fast to notice me there. There becomes home when you no longer crave carved monuments to strangers.

• • •

Santa Cruz was not my home when I moved there from Berkeley, hired to teach neo-hippies about neo-Indians and to write. The land is seductive but expensive, the sea is inviting but cold, the weather is pleasant but boring, and most of the people are in love with all the wrong things. I've endured their cultured taunts defaming midwestern lives and have wondered aloud whether I should quit this project. But the escape from homelessness came on a cool evening after I had put my things in storage and finished scrubbing down my vacant quarters. I conjured up the two women who displaced my dreams, and I revisited my dead-of-night walk away from self-destruction; I heard the birds sing in the eucalyptus one last time, and I found myself at home, in that moment, right there. There becomes home, don't you see, when your ineffable past catches up with you, when you're embraced by the singular beauty of remembering.

Every part of this soil is sacred in the estimation of my people. Every hillside, every valley, every plain and grove, has been hallowed by some sad or happy event in days long vanished.

Chief Seattle

James Treat is an assistant professor of American Studies at the University of California in Santa Cruz. He was born in Oklahoma, and lived in Kansas and South Dakota before moving to California for graduate study. He is an enrolled citizen of the Muscogee (Creek) Nation in Oklahoma.

A Place of Light

 I have lived in ten million homes. Some were as big as Jupiter, others tiny as the spots on a ladybug's back. They've been solid as stone and gossamer as the warp and weft of my dreams. I have had homes with roofs that leaked, cracks in the walls, and mice in the cupboards, but always the sun in the morning and starshine at night. I have had homes with nothing over my head except clouds and wind.

My homes have been places and times imbued with a profound feeling of connection, laced with affection. Like a good friend, each has nourished my spirit. No matter how brief our bond, they have given me refuge, the impalpable yet clear conviction that I was, if only for a heartbeat, somehow less vulnerable to the unpredictable chaos of the world because of them.

As, immutably, has this breathtaking planet. It is sustenance and protection, primal source and ultimate destination, the environment to which I am emotionally attached. With heart and body and soul I belong to this earth, as I belong to everything and everyone I love. It owns me, with a kind of benign possession. It is a place of light.

Lucy Aron is a writer and former songwriter. Her home sits on a knoll above Santa Barbara, California with a wide-angle view of the sea, her spiritual home. She is currently working on a novel about the information superhighway.

The attic comes from the architecture of the ancient Greeks. It was a design meant to give symmetry to buildings by adding another story decorated with columns and giving the building greater height.

Home Again

I climb the three flights of stairs and walk toward the door of my apartment. As I turn the key my breath comes out in a soft rush. The workday is done.

It is the same exhalation that I breathed out on certain Wednesdays when, instead of eating with the crowd of noisy children in the school cafeteria, I walked with my sisters to our grandfather's house. We watched him slice the loaf of heavy German pumpernickel against his chest in the darkened dining room. We ate slowly and answered his questions with few words.

That breath is the noisy sigh I gave when I crashed into the unlocked house after another endless day of high school and the breath that I kept bottled up during the day as a young teacher. Today the exhale continues as I put my bag of groceries on the kitchen counter and turn to my plants who look thirsty after waiting for me all day in the hot spring sun.

I am home.

Kathleen Byrne lives in San Francisco, where she works as a learning specialist and a publicist. She dreams of living and writing in the countryside of Marin County and is working on improving her discipline and attention span.

Imagine yourself on a winter afternoon with a pot of tea, a book, a reading light, and two or three huge pillows to lean back against. Now make yourself comfortable. Not in some way which you can show to other people, and say how much you like it. I mean so that you really like it, for yourself.

**Christopher Alexander,
from *Home: A Short
History of an Idea***

Ten Ways to Honor Your Spiritual Home

- Create a special spot in your house or garden to meditate or reflect about your spiritual home.

- Smash a sacrificial object once a year to remind yourself of the impermanence of material possessions and the permanence and enduring qualities of your spiritual home.

- Learn a story about your ancestors from an older family member and pass it on to a younger member of your tribe to keep alive the spirit of family.

- Imagine the most important things you would take from your house if you knew that an emergency was imminent and your house could be destroyed. Make a list.

- As you walk through your front door when you come home after work or school, remind yourself of your good fortune. To remind yourself, post a special symbol or picture on the door jamb or wall that you see as soon as you come inside.

- Imagine yourself homeless without any possessions and imagine what you would do to make yourself feel safe, clean, loved, and at home.

- Make a list of all the places you've lived. Describe what you treasure about each home and what you carried forward from home to home.

- When you hear of someone in your community who has lost a home to a natural disaster, write them a letter of sympathy.

- When you cleanse your body, remind yourself that this sturdy and fragile construction of chemicals and intricate cells somehow mysteriously lets you be here, at this moment, as you have been countless moments before. Clean it with care.

- Remind yourself that you are your own best home and that your feeling of home goes wherever you go.

RITUALS, BLESSINGS, AND MEDITATIONS

*The friends of the farm came to the house and went
away again. They were not the kind of people who stay for
a long time in the same place. They were not the kind of people
either who grow old. They died and never came back. But they had
sat contented by the fire and when the house, closing round
them said "I will not let you go except you bless me."
They laughed and blessed it. And it let them go.*

Isak Dinesen, *Out of Africa*

A WORD ABOUT RITUALS

As long as there have been homes, there have been blessings to protect and care for those who live within their sheltering walls. In past centuries, ancient people sought the kindness and benevolence of the gods to protect their homes. Whether palaces or rough huts, priests and shamans came to sanctify, to bless, to celebrate. Sometimes holy water was sprinkled over the doorstep, sometimes bread or wine were shared, special signs were painted on the house sides or sacred objects placed near the front door. No matter the tradition, the motivation was to thwart the threat from without and to promise a safe haven within.

The rituals included in this chapter derive their gestures from impulses as old as humankind—to be safe, to be sheltered, to be loved. These ceremonies are meant to be guides or patterns to give you a sense of how many different cultures and peoples bless their homes. You may wish to create your own blessing ritual and ceremony, to be used for a special occasion such as a housewarming or even annually as a renewal of spirit and love.

You may also wish to build a shrine or altar in your house or garden. For some, an altar with items from beloved and absent family members brings the comfort of their remembered presence. Altars can be a window for contemplative thought, with a picture of a mountain landscape or the unruffled surface of a lake to focus upon or the simplicity of a rounded granite rock to gaze at. Outside, altars seem to open the spirit to the cleansing of fresh air and the simple beauty of nature. Find a special platform to sit on, position a chair near an expansive view, or find the one spot in your garden where you cannot be seen by any of your neighbors and use that area for quiet contemplation. There is even an Eastern tradition of writing thoughts, haiku, or remembrances on strips of rice paper and fastening them to tree limbs to gently stir in the breeze. The wafting air seems to send the messages up to the gods while you observe the thought again and again as the paper floats in the air.

Approaching our homes with reverence and gratitude seems to be a natural outpouring of our thankfulness for their protection, rest, and comfort. Rituals tie us to our past, the long line of those who came before us, and seat us in the present, reminding us of the abundance of our good fortune. Lastly, rituals promise us the future, linking us with the anticipation of coming days and years. Blessing ceremonies with family and friends bring home the profound meaning of shelter—a sense of personal joy and a recognition of the love that houses us and protects us against the winds and storms of time and fortune.

A Housewarming Ritual

This ritual may be used any time you want to celebrate your home, whether you have just purchased or rented it, or have been living there for years. Perform it alone, or with friends, or family members. Try to perform it during daylight.

You will need a few simple tools: one beeswax or white candle, never before burned, and one smudge stick or incense stick. (Smudge sticks are bundles of sweet, dried herbs. You can purchase them at most New Age or metaphysical shops or make your own.) Find a beautiful feather—one you are willing to part with—and gather salt, preferably rock salt, and a loaf of bread that you have baked or at least symbolically heated up in the oven of the house you are warming.

Arrange your tools in any way that is beautiful to you on the floor or on a table. Then say the following words out loud:

We are here today to create our home. This dwelling, this collection of wood and nails and plaster and paint, possesses a spirit which today becomes part of our family. We welcome this home, embrace it, and trust it with our bodies and our hearts for as long as we live under this roof. We are grateful for the shelter and warmth it provides.

For as long as we live here, our cares will be as light as this feather. Our worries will float gently out of the window and away. (Open the window and let the feather drift away in the breeze.)

For as long as we live here, our path will be lit like the flame of this candle. Our home will shelter and protect us so the flame will burn ever bright and warm. (Light the candle.)

For as long as we live here, our lives will be full of flavor like this salt. Our home will hold it in unexpected places, offering it for our continuous delight. (Sprinkle the salt in the nooks and crannies of every room of your home.)

For as long as we live here, our souls will be nourished as we are nourished by this bread. We shall never hunger in body or spirit. (Take a few bites of the bread.)

For as long as we live here, our lives shall be filled with love as this smoke fills our home. Like this smoke, our love shall expand and permeate all of the rooms of this house. (Light the smudge stick and make a full circuit of the house with it.)

Our heartbeats, our breath, and our dreams join those of our home and of all the others who lived here before us. When one day we leave this home, we will leave a part of ourselves behind but shall carry a part of this home with us. We welcome our home into our family, and we joyfully await all of our tomorrows within its embrace.

Finally, take the still-lit smudge stick and circle around the outside of the house, laughing and singing and generally making merry.

As a real estate agent, **Holly L. Rose** has performed many housewarming rituals for friends and clients.

Taking Care of Our Hearts

As a Feng Shui practitioner, I believe that houses and homes sustain the human spirit and that physical environments can either take care of us or do us harm. My work helps people to see the patterns they have woven into their life, and whether or not those patterns suit them. By seeing the pattern without, they can see it within.

Once I was hired to look at the home of a husband and wife and their four-year-old daughter. Something was wrong at home especially at bedtime, and they asked if I could help. The mother's concern focused on a growing tension between herself and the child, attributing the nightly upset to her daughter's "childish" behavior.

As we moved through the house, I bumped into a bookcase in the hallway, and had to move quickly to save a beautiful crystal pyramid from hitting the floor. Lining the top of the bookcases were other beautiful pieces of artwork, pottery, and glassware—things that could break.

On the bottom of the bookcase were the little girl's toys. The bookshelf was not very steady, and each night when the little girl put her toys back on the bookshelf, it would wobble.

Nothing had ever fallen from the bookcase, but the daily possibility that some cherished object might fall was a constant aggravation. Bedtime became fraught with resentment, anger, and rebellion and a time of tension between the mother and the daughter.

I asked the mother if she could find another place to put her delicate pieces of art. I didn't even have to explain why. She looked at me and said, "I created this. I've created the conflict with my daughter, and I need to look within and see what it is that I can do to change this. And the first thing I can do is move my things, and let my daughter be four years old."

The words that we use in our home, the way we make the bed, the way we walk through the living room, the way we hold our babies—all of these actions affect the entire family. They change the hearts of everyone, and one heart touches another until the feeling is felt around the world.

This is why we all have a tremendous responsibility to act in a way that nurtures the heart. One healthy open heart can change the world. And home is the place to begin.

Katherine Metz draws on Native American, Hawaiian, and Chinese arts of healing and place to explore the seen and unseen ways that the physical environment, home, and workplace can spark and nurture an individual's natural potential. Blending her healing arts with a degree in medical sociology and design experience from her interior landscape firm, she has developed The Art of Place.

Nine Ways to Arrange for Good Fortune

Drawing on the ancient Chinese art of placement called Feng Shui, all of us can make simple and affordable changes in our homes and workplaces that will spark our natural potential and help bring clarity and peace, joy and prosperity. Here are nine simple ways to arrange for your good fortune.

- *For clarity, place a brass wind chime just inside your front door.*
- *For insight, place books where you will see them as you enter the house.*
- *For peace of mind and body, place your bed and your desk so that you can easily see the door. Avoid being in direct line with the door.*
- *To reduce stress, place two mirrors opposite one another so that you walk between them as you enter your home or office.*
- *To bring more love, compassion, and understanding to your relationship, hang a round mirror in your bedroom.*
- *To increase your prosperity, mirror the wall behind your stove, reflecting the burners, symbols of wealth and prosperity.*
- *To cultivate good luck, place flowers in the bedroom, study, and kitchen.*
- *To enhance your ability to move forward, move twenty-seven objects in your home which have not been moved in the last year.*
- *In times of difficulty, place yourself in the moonlight and breathe.*

Katherine Metz

A Protestant Episcopal Home Celebration

I was ordained to the priesthood in the Episcopal Church in 1982 and have used the Episcopal Church's Celebration for a Home many times in my ministry. I haven't just used it because it was there and should be used; rather I have used it because the homeowners really wanted the occasion, feeling a deep need to celebrate and to thank God for being present in all the moments and dwelling places of our ordinary days.

I have been asked to bless a home in which people have been living for years in order to ask God to grace it with the Easter promise of a new life. One of these occasions came about because of a happy reconciliation in a marriage; and another occurred when a suicide had cast gloom on a house; and still another welcomed a new baby.

I have twice used the service to bless my own homes, both times with the jovial participation of my Presbyterian husband. The ceremony made a tremendous difference to me each time.

In the service, an invocation is read, and the participants walk from room to room, with a lit candle, celebrating each room. I suppose I, or any Episcopalian, could write new prayers, but we usually choose not to. The familiar ritual of our traditional prayers allows us to move deeper than a mere intellectual grasp of words and phrases.

Reverend Dr. Louise Parsons Pietsch is the rector of St. Luke's Episcopal Church in Katonah, New York. Dr. Pietsch was ordained to the priesthood in 1982. She has three children and is married to the Reverend Dr. William V. Pietsch, a Presbyterian pastor.

Light of Truth, Science of Mind Blessing for the Home

Home once represented a place where I would go when there was no other place available, a structure, a place which held little meaning for me.

Now my home is a warm comforting place within myself that I turn to for all I need. Since I am a minister with Religious Science this makes sense, because we believe the kingdom of heaven is within each and every individual.

I came home when I realized God was not separate from me and because of my studies came to know that God is the central theme running through all things in this universe. In my church I teach what coming home is all about. No matter where I am and in whatever circumstances I may find myself, home is where I am.

I have been called upon to do many home blessings. Prayer is a vital part of the ceremony, and along with that I have at times used incense, candles, and blessed water, which lends a sense of ceremony and completion for the participants. I try to tailor the ceremony around what is important to the people. The invocation of the Holy Spirit is the most important thing because this consecrates the home and focuses on the principles of love, safety, security, protection, peace, and love, not only for the structure itself, but for the family members dwelling within. Here is a suggested home blessing.

A Home Blessing

The following procedure can be used by one individual or a hundred and one. If you wish, include your friends and new neighbors in your ceremony. It's a great time to become better acquainted with your neighbors, and after the blessing is a wonderful time to break bread together. Who knows, before long you may well be blessing the entire neighborhood.

As you go through the rooms, it is not necessary to have each individual repeat the same words. What is important is to say the affirmation out loud for the particular room, and others may respond with "Amen."

With your family and friends, stand outside the front door. Light a white candle for each person living in the house. (Candles contained in glass are safer.) If you have any children, involve them. Children love ceremonies, and this is their home also.

Give each person a candle. As you step over the threshhold say, "God bless this house, God bless my home." Have each person living in the house repeat this blessing as they enter. For those not living in the house, who are taking part in the ceremony, simply have them say "God bless this house" as they enter.

The living room: Gather in the main room and affirm, *"This room is blessed by God and is filled with love, joy, peace, and harmony. Amen."*

The dining room: *"This room is blessed by God and filled with love, where we share our blessings and give thanks for our bountiful supply. Amen."*

The kitchen: *"This room is blessed by God and is filled with love, harmony, and sustenance. Amen."*

A bedroom: *"This room is blessed by God and is filled with love, serenity, relaxation, peace, and safety. Amen."*

The bathroom: *"This room is blessed by God and filled with love, where we are cleansed, refreshed and made new. Amen."*

The office: *"This room is blessed by God and filled with love, creativity, and productivity. Amen."*

The den: *"This room is blessed by God and filled with love, wisdom, and relaxation. Amen."*

The garage: *"This area is blessed by God and filled with love, safety, and protection. Amen."*

The yard: *"This area is blessed by God and is filled with love, laughter, happiness, relaxation, safety, and joy. Amen."*

Gather back in the main room once again and say, *"My home is blessed by God and may all who enter know the love, happiness, safety, security, and protection this house affords. Thank you God. Amen."*

If you have additional structures you want blessed such as a guest house or shed, use the previous blessings as a foundation for continuing your ceremony. Don't forget the doghouse!

Reverend Leah Wise is a minister of the Light of Truth, Science of Mind Center in San Fernando, California, a suburb of Los Angeles. Reverend Leah's ministry involves the recognition and realization of our spiritual nature and application of this knowledge to daily living.

The Altar in the Temple of the Soul

The body is our first earthly home. We honor it as the temple of the soul; the chalice that contains the spiritual energies in the universe. It is the elixir of life and immortality that courses through the nerves and blood and energy pathways of this precious, complex, fragile, and incredible home. The heart is the altar of that temple.

It is through the heart energy, the sacred heart, the symbolic heart, that anger, resentment, pain, loss, and judgment are experienced and mysteriously transformed by the qualities of forgiveness, thankfulness, and compassion. The beauty of the soul is experienced through the expansion of the heart.

Let this beauty, peace, and serenity permeate the air where you walk. Release the sacred energies streaming through your heart to everything and everyone. Think of your heart as an altar, and realize that this altar goes wherever you go. Let its beauty be reflected in your home, the architectural extension of your self.

Building an altar in your home is an expression of homage to the divinity in you. Choose a special location, and begin by cleansing the space with water brought in from a holy source or made holy by intention and prayer. Purify the air with aromatic oils in the form of incense or essential oils dispersed by misting. Burn herbs and resins such as sage, mugwort, osha, frankincense, myrrh, or cedar. The spiritual energy of the plants and the intention of the ritual will invite the spirits of the land and of the traditions and will bless the household.

Gifts of the natural world at the altar will remind us of ourselves as elements of nature. Placing and floating flowers at an altar is particularly potent in working magic with their scent, color, and beauty. The water may be used for bathing and drinking as it has a purifying and calming effect. Some greenery and fruits may be added to signify vitality and abundance. Rocks, feathers, shells, crystals, or bones included in the altar represent the other qualities of the earth. Candles or oil lamps symbolize the flame of the sacred that burns in the depth of the soul. Photographs and artwork evoke both remembrance and inspiration.

The altar in your home is only a reminder and expression of the most meaningful aspects of your life at that time. As your life unfolds, so will your altar. The altar is a reflection of the inner self and the experience of the mystery of being. Listen for a symbolic message from deep within yourself. Listen to your heart, your home. Place objects from your daily life on the altar. Photographs and pictures can be added both for remembrance and for inspiration. Listen for a symbolic message from deep within yourself. Listen to your heart, your home.

Wai-Ching Lee is a holistic healer and counselor. Her work in personal and planetary transformation embraces the philosophy of mind, body, and spirit integration, using bodywork, movement, sound therapy, aromatherapy, and flower essences.

A Meditation on Home

To be at rest and joyful, to be peaceful and filled with loving kindness
is possible for every human being. Through our loving attention we can
awaken to this present moment, and we can discover our true home. Out-
wardly it does not matter whether our home is a large house where we are
surrounded by a loving family, a small apartment, or a temporary abode
while we travel. The spirit of being at home arises whenever our heart
rests in mindfulness and well-wishing. In that way we can create a home
wherever we are.

Everyday, try to find time to reflect…and meditate. Make yourself comfortable in a favorite spot—a special room, a favorite chair, or perhaps the
garden—wherever you feel most connected to your surroundings. Close your
eyes and let your body be at rest. Let your heart be open, releasing
the worries and tensions of the day. Notice your breath as you breathe in
and out. As you sit, let your thoughts and feelings rise and fall like the
waves of the ocean. Notice how you feel; notice the smells and the sounds
of your home; notice if you feel warm or cool. Then, as you become settled,
begin to recite the following words from your heart:

May I be peaceful and at ease

May my home be filled with loving kindness

May it be a safe haven

May I be happy

At home, in the present moment

This meditation may be used at home or away. If you rest in the present moment, you can be at home anywhere.

Jack Kornfield mows his lawn, gardens, and lives with his wife and daughter in Woodacre, California. He is a Buddhist meditation teacher and wrote *A Path with Heart* and *Buddha's Little Instruction Book,* among other books.

Nine Rituals to Celebrate Home

- Plan a house blessing. Invite your friends, family, and religious leader to lead a blessing ceremony in your home. If you prefer, make up your own ceremony using your favorite thoughts or poems. Fill the house with very fragrant flowers, light many, many candles, and have everyone bring food to share.

- Find a family heirloom, and place it so you notice it every time you walk into your house. Select a special dish, serving spoon, or platter and use it every family holiday meal, introducing the piece and tracing its heritage from family to family until it arrived at your table.

- Create a ritual to honor those family members who came before you. Make a family wall with photographs and label each one with the person's name and their date of birth. Write down all the family stories you can think of and ask any older relatives to tell you the family history. Toast your ancestors on Thanksgiving Day. Preface each toast by having family members recall an anecdote about a relative. Place objects from beloved relatives on a bookshelf, display cabinet, or mantel. Light a candle in remembrance of your ancestors.

- Cut off a piece of your Christmas tree or New Year's Eve log and save it to start next year's holiday fires. Design a special meal for a midnight feast on New Year's and only serve it once a year on that festive occasion.

- At a specific time you choose on a solstice day, mark where the sun's rays shine against your house or inside on your walls. Place a special mark or sign or hang a feather so you can recognize the sun approaching the solstice season after season.

- Learn one recipe for baking bread. On the day of summer solstice, bake a loaf of bread and share it with all your family to honor the generosity of Mother Earth. On winter solstice day, light a candle just as the sun sets to celebrate the lengthening of the days and the turning of the season.

- Write out your ideas of the hospitality and shelter that you want your house to offer your family and friends. Frame the finished version and hang the invocation in your kitchen or guest bedroom.

- Every year, renew your house blessing with a ceremony that marks the year passed with its misfortunes and fortunes. Take a moment to remember your blessings, and let everyone in your family tell the event of the year which brought to them the most joy.

- Celebrate personal dates of immense importance or intimate pleasures such as the day you first moved into your house, the day a family member died, the day a special food comes into season in your garden, the day the first migrating robin is sighted in the neighborhood. Make sure every family member has a task to perform and observe these without fail year after year.

Afterword

The contributors to this book have provided a wide spectrum of different perspectives on the meaning and experience of being at home. Anyone reading the writings collected here will appreciate more fully the vastness and mystery of the idea of "home," with its many levels of meaning. Yet is there a thread that can tie all these different perspectives together?

A common thread emerges if we consider home as a mandala. Mandalas are symbols of totality, portrayed in many different times and cultures as circles with four directions and a strong central focus. They are sacred structures that represent the cosmos in symbolic form. Cosmos literally means "orderly world." What is home, if not a place where we find or try to create order?

A mandala is sacred because it contains all the elements of creation within its order, including chaos. Like a mandala, home is also a sacred space, because it is where we can let ourselves be—the whole cosmos that we are, including all our inner chaos. It is where all the different parts of us can reside and be contained. Home is whatever holds, contains, nurtures, and protects the process of our unfolding as human beings.

This understanding helps clarify why home is so often considered sacred and why it can have so many different meanings for different people. For some it is a place, while for others it is a person or a sense of well-being.

Home is whatever promotes and fosters our development by providing a ground to stand on.

In the Buddhist tradition, mandalas function on three different levels—outer, inner, and secret. The outer aspect of a mandala is how it manifests—its form and structure. The inner aspect of a mandala is what goes on within it—its energetic qualities and felt meaning. And the secret or innermost aspect of a mandala is how it affects and acts on us in more subtle, less visible ways.

As an outer mandala, home is first and foremost a place: a beloved house, the lap of our family, the town where we grew up, a neck of the woods whose creatures, trees, weather, and moods imprinted themselves on our soul. For traditional peoples who lived closer to the earth, the land they inhabited provided that kind of holding container. Their whole world was home to them.

Compared with native peoples who were wedded to the land they inhabited, how can we rootless Americans ever hope to find this kind of home? We move every few years, from house to house, town to town, state to state. And when we go back to visit our childhood home, we often find that a developer has installed a strip mall where our favorite forest was, and our old brown-shingle house has been bulldozed to make way for a set of upscale condominiums.

Although America has learned to speed up the natural process of impermanence, the truth is that no home in this world is or could be permanent or stable. Most of the native people of this planet have by now been rudely turned out of their homes. Whatever house we currently call home will soon enough be inhabited by strangers, who will in turn call it their home. And in time our dear planet itself will disintegrate.

So we must look deeper. This brings us to the inner level of the mandala, where home is not just a place, but also an experience—of being held and nurtured—which provides a sense of belonging. On this level, we start to realize that home is not something outside us. Home is this sense of being connected—which certain beloved places and people help us to discover and feel. Being at home is a feeling of being grounded and at one with life —which allows us to relax and be ourselves. This home we can take with us wherever we go.

And yet, it is usually hard to feel this way all the time. Feelings continually change, just as places do. Even with those to whom we feel closest, there are times when we wonder if we really know them, if we really belong with them. Sometimes we even wonder if we belong here on this earth at all. Thus if we only rely on a positive sense of belonging to feel at home, we may live much of our lives in exile.

So once again, we must go deeper, and this brings us to the secret mandala —its innermost core, or true, ultimate meaning. Here we must pass beyond feeling and arrive at being—where we do not just feel at home, but we are at home. Yet where is that? Where is it that we really are at home, regardless of all the vagaries of impermanence?

Our true home ground cannot be anything but who we really are. Anything else—including who we think we are—is bound to shift and slip out from under our feet. When we look deeply into who we are, we discover a nameless, formless presence that is awake, open, and responsive to life. This is our true nature, our being or essence, also known in various traditions as the true self, holy spirit, or buddha-nature. This is what truly holds, contains, nurtures, and protects us when all else fails. It is our true ground, the ground of being.

This placeless place is truly "where the heart is." In the Eastern traditions, the word heart means "core," "pith," "essence." Thus home is where our essential nature is, our very source. This is a home we do not need to build or fabricate—how could we fabricate what we already are? We only need to discover it, for it is already present within us. As the Indian sage H. L. Poonja asks: "How much time does it take to go home when you are already sitting at home?"

The open presence at the heart of our being is the only place we can come back to again and again, wherever we are.

John Welwood, Ph.D., is a clinical psychotherapist in San Francisco, associate editor of the Journal of Transpersonal Psychology, and a leading figure in the field of East/West psychology. His books include the best-selling *Journey of the Heart: Intimate Relationship and the Path of Love* and *Ordinary Magic: Everyday Life as Spiritual Path.*

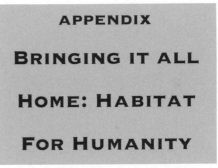

APPENDIX

Bringing it all Home: Habitat For Humanity

If there is harmony in the house,
  There will be order in the nation.
If there is order in the nation,
  There will be peace in the world.

Chinese Proverb

Home as Habitat

This book has come together like a house, with many nails, many beams, many windows, many people contributing to make a whole from parts. We have learned from our contributors that a home means much more than four walls. But in our society, starting with four walls and a roof means sharing in basic values, being a part of our society in a way that recognizes and celebrates the human spirit bonded together in community.

Habitat For Humanity has recognized this basic need, and as an organization it quietly works with volunteers, private donations, and communities to build a fellowship of participants that fosters home ownership with pride and responsibility.

Habitat For Humanity International has over 1,000 affiliates worldwide and has built more than 30,000 houses to shelter families in nearly forty countries. Working together to create strong neighborhoods and healthy communities, mothers and fathers, children and single people, architects, doctors, lawyers, college students, secretaries, and church groups, among others, join together to provide homes and home ownership. This disparate group of home builders shares the common vision that everyone should have a home to call their own.

These houses are not given away as acts of charity. The homeowners put in at least 500 hours of sweat equity—they bring their hopes home by actually building their own house, timber by timber, room by room, and cabinet by cabinet. Family members help out by working in the Habitat office, digging ditches for the sewer lines in their house, and building closets and installing windows. The families visit the building site whenever they can, coming to hammer, to scramble over the roof to lay out sheets of roofing, or just to walk through the skeleton of their own home, seeing their dreams becoming real in front of their eyes. The homeowners pay off their no-interest mortgages, knowing that every dollar they pay back goes into the building fund to finance homes for other families.

Habitat families include people of all races, all religious persuasions, all walks of life. Habitat teaches all these people to work together with many other volunteers and candidate families in coordinated teams. Each person learns how to build a home in cooperation with others. The skills they learn as they build underlie the pride of their accomplishments and support the lifelong task of maintaining their houses with pride and dignity.

In all of this, a home is something everyone has in common. Everyone from Africa to America understands the meaning of living in a home. Whether a Mongolian yurt, an Eskimo igloo, or a Wisconsin log cabin, no matter how small or how large, whether sharing walls in noisy bustling cities or standing alone on the crest of a hill, a home stands for the spirit of individuality, the love of family, the web of community.

As we researched this book, we talked to many committed volunteers and participants who have made Habitat For Humanity a way of life. We found their stories inspiring and hopeful.

The Editors

Home and Hope

 We bought a starter home in West Oakland, California. It needed a lot of work, but we thought that after putting some time in working on the house we could sell it and buy a bigger house when our children got older. But all those dreams came to an end after the Loma Prieta earthquake hit the San Francisco Bay Area in 1989.

The evening of the earthquake we were forced to move out of our house because it was not safe. We locked up the house, but soon people began to break in and steal our belongings. We kept going back to secure the house, but after a few days they would break in again. Finally, everything we owned was gone. Our only hope was that we would be able to move back into the house, but then we discovered we couldn't because the cost of the repairs was so high and we didn't have the money and couldn't borrow it.

After that, we went through some very difficult times. It was a year of continual loss, and we lived through it by operating out of a survival mode—just living day by day. I lost my job because the place where I worked was also severely damaged by the earthquake. It was very hard on us, and we had no hopes or dreams left. We only had enough energy to do what was absolutely necessary to get through the next day. The only plans for the future

As a builder, it is particularly gratifying to build something that is needed—not just wanted. Even more pleasing is the opportunity to work with the volunteers we see every week. At the construction sites, a rhythm develops. The hammers rise and fall. The people come and go. We discover needs and the needs are met. The neighborhood changes bit by bit and I am filled with hope. I think that's why people are drawn here. Habitat provides hope.

Roger Rushing
Construction Supervisor

we made were for the kids, getting them enrolled in their schools.

We wanted to stay in the Bay Area, because it was our home, but it is a very expensive place to live and we thought we would never again be able to raise enough money to buy a house here. Our desire to own our own home was so strong that we even toyed with the idea of moving to other places.

Shortly after the earthquake, we heard that Habitat For Humanity was active in the Bay Area. We got an application, filled it out and submitted it. We didn't hear from them until two years later when they called and asked us if we would like to become candidates for a home.

From the day they called, Habitat For Humanity became synonymous with home and hope for us. When we became home-owner candidates, we began to think about being in a home again and how it would affect our lives. Planning for our new home stabilized us. Hope came back into our lives. As part of the Habitat program, we were able to move into reconditioned apartments right across from the building site of our new home. It's been really fun to watch the progress on our home. Seemingly a symbol of good things to come, one week after we heard from Habitat I got a job and can support my family again.

Vernell Davis

I'm beginning to understand that if community action is to be truly viable it must, at its core, be derived from a complete and true sense of home… beginning in the heart, activated throughout a household and then spreading from neighbor to neighbor, and community to community.

Hiroko Kurihara
Habitat Staff

185

For a long time I couldn't even listen to our story without it bringing tears to my eyes. The kids would beg me to go and see our old house, but I couldn't even drive past it. It wasn't until Habitat called us that I could drive by the house and look at it. Now I tell myself that one day I'm going to have my home again, I'm going to build it myself and my kids are going to help. One day someone asked my son if he wanted a job. He looked at the guy and said "I already have a job. I work for Habitat For Humanity." I was very proud of him. We've committed our lives to Habitat because it started us again and brought us to a home. We've finished putting in our required five hundred hours of work on our home, but we want to help others build their own even after we've moved into our own home.

Larri Ann Davis

Vernell and Larri Ann Davis and their three children are looking forward to settling into their new home in February 1995.

The community process at Habitat For Humanity yields innumerable benefits to the individual as people come together and work toward a common goal.

Joel T. Mackey
Executive Director,
East Bay Habitat
For Humanity

Building Community

 I got involved with the local branch of Habitat For Humanity by making a contribution to the national organization. I admired the way the organization runs itself, with homeowners paying their mortgages and those payments financing the next houses in their neighborhood. I started volunteering for them because I shuffle papers at my job all week, and at the end of the week the only accomplishment I can see is that a pile of papers that was in the in-box has moved to the out-box. After a Saturday working at Habitat, I can see a whole new second story on a house and know that I have built a closet, set in a window, or hung a door. I can really see that I have accomplished something important—building a home for people.

Habitat brings people from different communities together, people whose paths would normally never cross. One day I was assigned to work on a project with two kids. Fish had a mohawk haircut, and Jesus had homemade tattoos on his arms. At first we just stared at each other—a middle-aged white woman and two young guys. As the day progressed, Fish taught me how to blunt my nails, and Jesus showed me how to stagger them on a two-by-four so that the board never splits. By the end of the afternoon we had finished our assignment and the three of us were friends.

All my life I wanted to have my own house —my own picket fence, my own walls. I wanted a home in which my children could grow. Habitat For Humanity builds houses, and it also builds lives, families, communities and self-esteem. Home is the real thing, and Habitat helped us get one.

Kareen Hunter
Habitat Homeowner

187

Now when I see a young man with a mohawk, I think differently about him than I would have before. I hope that Fish and Jesus look at middle-aged white women differently too.

Habitat creates community. A few Saturdays on the job and I get to know a new neighborhood, one I would never have driven through, much less spent time in, before I worked with Habitat. Now I know the neighbors and the kids, and I feel like I'm a part of a different neighborhood in my community. Thanks to Habitat For Humanity, I feel that we share a common purpose and a common goal.

Every Saturday **Susan Frank** delivers a basket of freshly baked muffins to the construction crew building houses for East Bay Habitat For Humanity. She takes off her apron, puts on her tool belt, and spends the rest of the day building.

I never lived in a "home home," a house "home." As a child, our family rented flats, so we always lived either under somebody or on top of somebody. With the help of Habitat For Humanity I will be the first woman in our family to own a home. And I know with the skills I've learned at the construction sites at which I've worked that I will be able to take good care of my house. I love going to work and telling my co-workers, "you are not going to believe this…I just wired a bedroom!" That makes me feel really good.

Cynthia Gentry
Habitat Candidate

Part of the Solution

 Habitat For Humanity has become a way of life for me. I try to show up every Saturday so I can work with my hands and with a variety of people.

During the week, I am an architectural designer, and I work inside all day, sitting at a computer or dealing with committees for large projects. I love construction, but to work at it professionally I would have to join a union and work full-time. Volunteering for Habitat every weekend leaves me with a six-day work week and really cuts into my free time, but I feel that I get back a lot more than I give.

I never know who I will work with; on any given Saturday I may meet a single mom or a physicist. The business of architecture can seem very isolated from people at times, so it's very rewarding for me to work directly at providing personal space and shelter for all kinds of people in all kinds of situations.

I think about my friend Verne and his kids, working and playing in the house they are building and getting ready to move into their home. I realize how lucky I have been in my family, my childhood, and my own home in San Francisco. Habitat has taught me to appreciate what I have and that I have something to give.

A home needs to be a loving environment. A loving environment

Home is the key to a healthy society. It's within the walls of our houses where we begin to learn how to interact with others and how to be a part of something larger than ourselves. As we grow older, our world expands from our home to our local community. Habitat contributes to this process by working with local communities and by providing safe, well-built and affordable homes.

Lori Jensen
Habitat Staff

189

in a home creates a sense of community that multiplies exponentially as it spreads to the larger community outside. As I learn a skill, I pass it on to someone else, and they in turn teach someone else. One individual's Saturdays may be very little, but they help me to see myself as part of the solution and to know that I am doing work that needs to be done.

Christopher Steward is a designer for an architectural firm. Born in Indiana, he has traveled all over the country.

We've waited for five years for our home. It's being built from the ground up. I think I'll be happy paying the mortgage and not paying someone else rent to pay someone else's mortgage. It will be nice to have the responsibility of having our own home. Habitat For Humanity is like a dream come true.

A. Lateefah Shaheed
Habitat Homeowner

Become a "Home Builder"

Want to help? If you can't pick up a hammer and some nails to build a house for your neighbors, do the next best thing: become a "home builder." By making a contribution to East Bay Habitat For Humanity, you can help us put one family in their own home.

A percentage of the profits from the sale of this book will be donated to East Bay Habitat For Humanity, located in Oakland, California. Together, brick by brick, dollar by dollar, we can make a difference. Joining in the joyous task of an old-fashioned "house raising," together we will all cross the threshold home.

Here is what your contribution to East Bay Habitat For Humanity will build:

$20.00 builds a front step
$50.00 builds a threshold
$100.00 builds a window
$240.00 builds a front door
$600.00 or more makes you a partner

Send your checks to: East Bay Habitat For Humanity
Department B
2619 Broadway
Oakland, California 94612
510 251-6304 or FAX 510 251-6309

East Bay Habitat For Humanity will put you on a mailing list to receive progress reports as they raise enough money to build a home.

If you would like to learn more about Habitat For Humanity or would like to become a volunteer, call the international office toll-free at 1-800-HABITAT to find the affiliate nearest you, or contact one of the regional offices listed below.

Habitat East (District of Columbia, Maryland, Virginia, West Virginia): P.O. Box 1403 Harrisonburg, VA 22801; 703 564-0556.

Habitat Heartland (Arkansas, Kansas, Missouri, Nebraska): P.O. Box 8955, Springfield, MO 65801-8955; 800 284-0982.

Habitat Mid-Atlantic (Delaware, New Jersey, Pennsylvania): P.O. Box 4984, Lancaster, PA, 17604-4984; 717 399-9592.

Habitat Mideast (Indiana, Ohio): 3130 Mayfield Rd., Suite 310 E, Cleveland, OH 44118; 216 321-0800.

Habitat Midwest (Illinois, Michigan, Wisconsin): 1920 South Latlin, Chicago, IL 60608; 800 643-7845.

Habitat Northeast (Connecticut, Maine, Massachusetts, New Hampshire, New York, Rhode Island, Vermont): P.O. Box 2322, Acton, MA 01720; 508 486-4421.

Habitat Northwest (Alaska, Idaho, Montana, Oregon, Washington): 1005 NW Galveston, Bend, OR 97701; 503 383-4637.

Habitat South (Alabama, Louisiana, Mississippi): P.O. Box 112, Tupelo, MS 38802-0112; 800 283-2397.

Habitat South Atlantic (North Carolina, South Carolina): P.O. Box 1712, Easley, SC 29640; 803 855-1102.

Habitat South Central (Kentucky, Tennessee): 248 East Short Street, Lexington, KY 40507; 800 865-7614.

Habitat Southeast (Florida, Georgia): 226 N. Laura Street, Jacksonville, FL 32202-3502; 904 353-1366.

Habitat Southwest (Oklahoma, Texas): P.O. Box 3005, Waco, TX 76707; 800 274-8177.

Habitat Upper Midwest (Iowa, Minnesota, North Dakota, South Dakota): P.O. Box 23316, Minneapolis, MN 55423-0316; 800 289-7872.

Habitat West (California, Nevada, Arizona, Hawaii): 534 22nd Street, Suite 209, Oakland, CA 94612; 510 286-8960.

Rocky Mountain Habitat (Colorado, New Mexico, Utah, Wyoming): 1331 East 31st Avenue, Denver, CO 80205; 303 296-0978.

Washington, DC Office: 1511 K Street, NW, Washington, DC 20005; 202 628-9171.

Author Index

Wildcat Canyon Press and New World Library are dedicated to publishing books and audio cassettes that help improve the quality of our lives. For a catalog of our fine books and cassettes, contact:

New World Library
Wildcat Canyon Press
14 Pamaron Way
Novato, CA 94949

Or call toll free:
(800) 227-3900

The text was set in 12 point Bodoni Book on 17 leading.

Interior and cover design by Sharon Smith Design.
Production by Lory Poulson and Susan Gluck.

Printed by Data Reproductions Corporation,
Rochester Hills, Michigan.